Praise for *A Way*

As a former missionary who lost a loved one while serving on the foreign mission field, I wish I'd had this book to help me through my own process of grief. Honest and authentic, *A Way in the Wilderness* not only gives readers permission to grieve, it also provides practical help through grief's journey. It is a must-read for anyone who needs a reminder of the hope in Christ after experiencing the sudden death of a loved one.

— Karen Miller
Former missionary to North Africa

A Way in the Wilderness can help us accept our brokenness and transform our fears. In telling her story, which is set against the beautiful backdrops of Mexico and Colorado, Rachel brings to light treasures of insight out of her experiences facing grief and devastation. This book is risky and honest. I loved it.

— Ferree Hardy
Author of Postcards from the Widows' Path

From the moment I started reading this book, I could not stop. The detailed and vivid descriptions placed me at each scene with the author. I was impacted by the rollercoaster of emotions Rachel felt in the face of tragedy. I also felt the arms of God wrap around her as He began to walk with Her through healing.

— Annette Bouadi
Pediatric Nurse

Rachel has written a beautiful narrative about the journey through suffering, loss, and renewal. I have often lamented that the Church in the west doesn't have a theology of suffering. And while this book is not an attempt to write such a theological treatise, it is written by a companion on the journey. Rachel writes out of her deep faith and scriptural undergirding in a way that makes profound truths accessible to one and all. Regardless of the nature of your brokenness and pain, in these pages you will find solace for your soul as you journey toward healing and restoration.

*— **Henry Yoder***
Pastor, Author of Longing for Eden

Profound, precise, and unabashedly honest, *A Way in the Wilderness* takes readers on an unforgettable journey down the harsh road of grief and into the Biblical understanding of loss. Will we allow ourselves to truly heal in all senses of the word, or remain steadfast in the grip of tragedy? *A Way in the Wilderness* reveals the healing reality of the power of Christ that is available to all of us.

*— **Billy Fraser***
Songwriter/Musician

A Way in the Wilderness took me on an emotional journey through the beautiful streets of Taxco and down the heartbreaking road of grief. As I read Rachel's story, I almost felt as if I were there with her. I wept. I laughed. I felt joy. I felt great sorrow. And ultimately, I saw the hope of God's promises. A must-read for anyone who has experienced great loss or simply wants to be inspired by God's work in a seemingly hopeless time.

*— **Amanda Dornsbach***
Interior Design Professional

Rachel shares her journey through the hardest season of her life with honesty and an openness that points to God's grace, love, and healing in the midst of dealing with the sudden loss of her husband. She reminds us there is hope even in hopelessness. I thoroughly recommend this book to anyone who has lost a husband.

— *Karen Wales*
Widow, Health Care Provider

As you walk the streets of the Mexican barrio with this precious missionary couple, you can't help but be drawn into their powerful story. In sharing the intimate details of her loss, Rachel exposes both the pain and the promise of grief. Rachel's remarkable story will propel every reader toward God's promise and hope for the future.

— *Rachel Lara*
Worship and Media Associate Radiant Church

Rachel's deeply transparent writing offers an invitation to step into years marked by deep pain and tremendous grace, and to glean wisdom born out of great sorrow and intense wrestling with the Lord. By fusing together personal testimony, thoughtful Biblical insight, and a Spirit-wrought joyfulness, Rachel's book serves as a gentle and powerful invitation to better know and walk with the God of all comfort.

— *Hannah Thompson,*
Director of Young Adults Ministry,
One Way Ministries

A WAY
in the
WILDERNESS

A Journey Through Grief & Grace

A WAY
in the
WILDERNESS

RACHEL A. MOORE
Foreword by Dick Eastman

A WAY
in the
WILDERNESS

Copyright © 2020 by Rachel A. Moore

Unless otherwise noted, scriptures are taken from the Holy Bible, New International Version®, NIV®. Copyright © 1973, 1978, 1984, 2011 by Biblica, Inc.™ Used by permission of Zondervan. All rights reserved worldwide. www.zondervan.com The "NIV" and "New International Version" are trademarks registered in the United States Patent and Trademark Office by Biblica, Inc.™

The views and opinions expressed in this book are those of the author and do not necessarily reflect the official policy or position of Illumify Media Global.

Published by
Illumify Media Global
www.IllumifyMedia.com
"We bring your book to life!"

Library of Congress Control Number: 2021900560

Paperback ISBN: 978-1-947360-80-8
eBook ISBN: 978-1-947360-81-5

Typeset by Art Innovations (http://artinnovations.in/)
Cover design by Bethany C. Moore

Printed in the United States of America

Dedication

In honor of Gary J. Moore, my beloved husband and dearest friend.
Your passion for grace and truth continues to be your legacy that pours out
of my life and through the pages of this book. The gratitude, admiration,
and respect that I feel for you is unending.

Contents

Acknowledgments

Bethany, my daughter, my inspiration! I could not have accomplished writing this book without you. I admire how you captured the message of hope in my book and depicted it beautifully in the illustration that you created for the cover. You are an incredibly talented artist and writer, and I am so blessed to have you as my daughter.

Nathaniel and Dorie, my dear son and daughter in-law: It's amusing that we both chose 2020 to accomplish noteworthy life achievements, you with your marriage and me in writing my book. Thank you for your grace and love toward this mother of the groom who had her head buried in her computer for most of the year. I love you both tremendously, and I am deeply grateful for the impact that you have had on my life and on my writing as well.

Andrea, my dearest friend: The pages of this book are dripping with God's message and anointing because of your prayers. I deeply appreciate the sacrifice of intercession on my behalf, and I humbly and gratefully share with you any eternal reward that may come from this book. I value your friendship beyond measure.

Karen, my editor and friend: When I met you at the Writers on The Rock conference in January 2020, I had no idea how deeply our lives would intertwine in the coming months as you walked me through the editing process on this book. During our many Zoom meetings, I entrusted my heart to you along with every chapter, be it humorous, bittersweet, or heart-wrenching. Professionally you are a talented writer and editor, but you are also a dear friend. I could not have entrusted the story of my husband's death to anyone else. I am profoundly grateful for you.

I also want to honor Max, who inspired me to become a writer. Your encouragement has given me the persistence and tenacity to write with excellence and complete my book. You have profoundly influenced my life for good. I am forever grateful.

And finally, I want to give praise, honor, and gratitude to Jesus.

My heart resonates with the words of the psalmist: "Not to us, LORD, not to us, but to your name be the glory, because of your love and faithfulness" (Psalm 115:1 NIV).

Foreword

Every follower of Christ will one day face wilderness encounters that, in the moment, may seem utterly hopeless. Yet amid unspeakable grief and utter despair, in seasons of disappointment and loss, God will always provide a way through.

In *A Way in the Wilderness*, Rachel Moore documents with unusual transparency and candid insights how to navigate these seasons of loss and despair. And in the process, she prepares us for our own journeys "from unimaginable heartbreak to unspeakable joy."

Over the years I have read many moving accounts written by those who have journeyed from tragedy to triumph, accounts I wished every follower of Christ would read. *A Way in the Wilderness* is surely at the top of that list.

Don't miss this remarkable narrative of heartache, hope—and the ultimate healing of a broken heart.

Dick Eastman
President
Every Home for Christ

Introduction

A few weeks after my husband's horrific death in southern Mexico, I awakened early. My dazed and sleepy mind gradually grasped the sweet melody of the tropical birds and the pungent fragrance of guava trees.

I stumbled to our kitchen, and a few minutes later, over a cup of coffee, I began to quietly pour my heart out to the Lord in prayer.

"Oh, God, what am I to do? How am I to survive without my husband? It's not fair! It wasn't supposed to be this way! We are on the mission field. My life feels totally barren and desolate."

I stared through a wall of windows into the surrounding jungle as the sun rose over the mountains and began to bring definition to the tropical foliage. In those moments, God spoke the promises from Isaiah clearly to my heart. His voice was loving and restorative in nature.

"I am about to do something new. See, I have already begun! Do you not see it? I will make a pathway through the wilderness. I will create rivers in the dry wasteland" (Isaiah 43:19 NLT).

Since Gary had died, there had not been one moment in which I had not felt gut-wrenching pain and the complete annihilation of life as I had known it. I was stunned to hear God's words of hope only weeks after my husband's death.

At that time, my life was a wilderness in every sense of the word. I desperately needed the Lord's rivers of life flowing through the desolation that death had created.

I left my coffee and got up from my place of prayer. I walked to one of the windowpanes that my husband had replaced during our renovation project. Where he had grasped the pane of glass, I could still see the faint outline of his fingerprints. I softly placed my fingers on the glass where his had been and wept.

I trusted in God's cathartic words even when I couldn't feel his presence or envision any hope for my future.

The loving picture God wants to show us, from Genesis to Revelation, is full of restoration and grace. But this restoration and grace is not instantaneous. There are many rocky hills we must climb and agonizing valleys of grief we must traverse.

Along the way, God's grace and love flows into our lives, and He creates rivers of abundance and healing where there had only been death and destruction.

Perhaps you have experienced an untimely or traumatic loss of your own.

If so, I promise that in the pages of this book I will share with you the experience of loss, but I will not leave you there alone and bewildered. My arm will wrap around you, and I will walk with you through your own journey of grief.

You will discover how to find freedom from the intensity of pain that sucker punches us after a loved one dies. You will find comfort in shared feelings and struggles.

It's also possible that you have picked up this book because someone you love is grieving, and you long to understand and support them on their journey. In these pages, you will find hope and healing to offer others.

Whatever your circumstances, I pray this book blesses you as you navigate the wilderness that is created by loss. May God's abundant rivers of healing and grace flow in and through you, transforming barrenness into abundant beauty.

One

THE HARBINGER OF GRIEF

"'As the Father has sent me, even so I am sending you.'"

John 20:21

My husband Gary and I sat together on the front stairs, our gaze lingering on the purple bougainvillea framing the wrought iron gate of our home and ministry center in southern Mexico.

As it did every morning, the strong sweet smell of the surrounding guavas wafted through the air. The monsoons had produced abundant tropical flowers, songbirds, and foliage but as is often the case, even good things can have a downside.

For us, it was our disagreeable roommates.

We had lived in southern Mexico for a year and a half with constant contention between ourselves and some unwanted residents in our home.

These unsavory characters had hairy legs and ominous shiny eyes, and leapt at our face when provoked. They crept stealthily on eight legs into my presence on a regular basis.

Eventually, I was able to offer a halfhearted greeting, mumbling "Oh. . . it's you, again," before going on with what I had been doing.

In this way, we developed a type of respectful friendship with the many tropical insects, arachnids, and animals who visited our home.

One of our favorite guests by far was the bright green motmot bird. He often sat in the mango tree by the front door, switching his tail back and forth in perfect rhythm to a jungle beat only he could hear.

Our children, fourteen-year-old Nathaniel and thirteen-year-old Bethany, were frequently eager to extend hospitality to these uninvited residents. Life in southern Mexico, for our young teenagers, seemed like a scene in an adventurous movie in which they enthusiastically played their part.

At least this was the case until one shadowy evening when a raccoon–like creature snuck quietly up the iron spiral stairs and padded into the bedroom where Nathaniel and Bethany were watching a movie.

"Mum!" Bethany screamed.

"No! Get out!" Nathaniel yelled, with as much manly authority as his fourteen years could fabricate.

"Nathaniel! Get him!" Bethany commanded her brother.

Gary and I heard the ensuing skirmish from our bedroom and abandoned conversational intimacy mid-sentence. Dashing up the circular stairs, Gary smacked his head on the spiral metal steps that had been built for the smaller stature of a Latino man.

My legs started to shake as I ran up the steps wondering what criminal had invaded my children's bedroom. We never thought of our own protection—our one consuming focus was Nathaniel and Bethany's safety.

As we neared the top of the staircase Gary and I could see the floor of Bethany's bedroom. Our eyes were riveted upon our children as we topped the stairs and rushed into the room.

"What happened?" Gary demanded, straightening his glasses from the impact on the stairs.

"Man, you guys terrified me." I said, holding back tears and feeling the relief of seeing two blond heads that had not been mangled by a drug cartel's blade.

Still shaking, I pushed aside the bowl of popcorn and sat down on Bethany's bed.

"It's okay, Mum." Bethany said, "It was a coatimundi."

"We saw his black eyes shining as he came up the stairs and that's when we started yelling at him," Nathaniel said, with the excitement of a teen boy on an epic adventure.

Bethany snuggled up to me. "He just kept coming at us and didn't seem to care that we were screaming."

"That's when I grabbed my mag light and shined it in his face," Nathaniel added boldly.

"He didn't care about our yelling, but he took off out the window when Nathaniel shined the light in his eyes. That part was funny," Bethany admitted, "but it was really scary at first."

Gary bopped Nathaniel on the head. "We'll start working on building screens as soon as I find the materials at the hardware store."

"Coatis are cute, but I don't like them staring at me in the dark with their big black eyes," Bethany said.

Gary pushed aside his gray hair and was cognizant of the bump on his head. "With the number of them that we have seen, I think a lot of the piles of poop that we found in the house may not have been from rats but from the coatis. They were probably living here before we started our renovations."

I stood up, trying to achieve normality. "I never thought of that, but you have a point."

Gary took my arm. "Rachel, are you okay?"

"Yeah, I'm fine, just a bit shaken," I responded in a half truth.

"Are you guys going to keep watching your movie?" Gary asked.

"Yeah, I think so," Nathaniel said turning to Bethany. "But let's leave a light on this time."

Bethany reached over the stack of books and turned on her bedside lamp. "Good idea. I don't want to go through that again."

Back in the comfort of our bedroom, Gary and I were able to chuckle at this unexpected adventure. Gary pulled me close and said, "I don't know why they wouldn't share their popcorn with the coati."

I fell into his arms laughing and shaking my head at the constant necessity of vigilance in the mountains of Mexico.

The steep serpentine streets of Taxco (pronounced Täs-co) were constructed after the conquest by Cortez and his invading troops. The multi-hued cobblestones provided traction for the donkeys who were loaded with supplies as the Spanish colonized southern Mexico. Today they reveal the mestizo passion for colorful beauty.

Our feet had grown to know these streets intimately over the past year and half since we had moved to Taxco from our home in Colorado. One thing that had struck us right from the beginning was the constant disparity between pristine beauty and defilement. On our first long treks through the city we had marveled at the delicate and alluring architecture, while wincing at the foulest sewer stench.

Eventually, all the sights and sounds—and even smells—blended together in a swirl of remembrance that would poignantly linger in our hearts for years to come.

Often, instead of walking we took a bumpy ride on the neighborhood *combi* bus. The passenger vans were always crammed full of fathers going to work, mothers of all ages nursing babies at exposed breasts, and joyful children piled on the floor occupying every inch of space. To accommodate more people, the sliding doors of the *combi* were permanently tied open with no consideration of safety.

We rarely sat together as a family but instead found any available space where our bodies could wedge in between the cluster of people traveling with us.

Bethany often clung to the edge of her seat closest to the open doorway while the road rushed past just a few feet away. She was less fearful of being catapulted from the moving vehicle than accidentally bumping into a random boy on the crowded bus. She would stare into the distance with a reflective expression letting the cool mountain air blow blond curls from her face. I often wondered at her introverted thoughts and what imaginary lands she had been visiting.

Always on the *combi* I saw alluring Latina women. These women of Taxco amazed me. I had come to the city wearing hikers with tread as deep as a tractor tire. I had been proud and ready to conquer the steep hills as if I were on a mountain trail in Colorado. But many of the Latina ladies of Taxco wore tight skirts, low–cut blouses, and high heels.

When we first arrived and I'd seen these provocative women traveling on the *combi*, I had looked at them with a smug certainty that when they got off, I would witness their wobbling ankles and four–inch narrow heels getting caught between the cobbles.

I'd been so wrong.

Now, my respect soared each time I saw them walking as fast and confidently in their sexy heels as I did in my Colorado army boots. I would never again question their abilities.

Every narrow winding street seemed like a work of art with beautiful structures on either side. The whitewashed houses were adorned with flowers and beautiful plants that offset red tiled roofs. Intricate baroque architecture was evident in the churches that were built throughout the city during the early 1500s. The bells of these cathedrals have rung for centuries and continue their infinite peal.

Frank Sinatra wrote the song "Sunrise over Taxco" and crooned of her loveliness. Anyone who has had the privilege of sauntering down the ancient streets undoubtedly understands Sinatra's adoration.

However, despite the ornate churches, the lush tropical mountains, and the warmth of the local people there is a confusing dichotomy between ancient and modern, innocent and corrupt, loving and hateful. The town is reminiscent of a small village in Italy where time seems to stand still.

Yet does it?

Is it pious or vile?

Taxco is in Guerrero which is a state burdened with drug cartel gang wars. It is not uncommon to hear of shootouts in the surrounding mountain locations. The people are subjected to brutal murders, criminal drug deals, and infiltrating corruption. Conversely, the town is world renowned for its exceptional art, costly silver, and the Holy Week processions since its inception in the 1500s.

Tourism is Taxco's main revenue and while we heard a lot of German, French, and Italian being spoken by visitors, precious few Americans seemed willing to risk the travel alerts. The fear of drug cartels kept most of our compatriots from vacationing in this distant region of Mexico and fewer still with the desire to live within the borders of the state of Guerrero. Because we were the only Americans in the area, we were an anomaly, and the locals welcomed us with openness and friendship.

Gary and I were seasoned in years but not as missionaries or world travelers.

Our relationship had begun nineteen years earlier in the suburbs of Pittsburgh, Pennsylvania. Gary had been leading numerous Bible study classes within our church as well as the annual fall retreats. At the same time, I was facilitating mission trips to Mexico City and hosting cross-cultural studies in my home.

The depth of our friendship developed into a passionate love that quickly led to marriage, despite the fact that he was eighteen years older than me.

A passion for ministry and a heart for Bible teaching formed the foundation of who we were as a couple. It was this drive that had brought Gary and me and our two middle-school-aged children from our life in Colorado into the heart of drug cartel–ruled southern Mexico.

Our love for the local people had steadied us as we survived the initial culture shock, and the natives honored our family because we had put ourselves at risk to come live among them and adopt their homeland as our own.

We did not show up as American experts ready to teach them our ways; instead, we humbled our hearts and desired to learn from them.

Nevertheless, the past eighteen months had been far from easy. Our family had experienced considerable adjustments as missionaries in a foreign country. Major illnesses, language struggles, cultural adjustments—all while trying to maintain a semblance of normality in our family life—had been daily challenges as soon as we'd crossed the Rio Grande.

I'll never forget our first few days living in Taxco. We moved into a small studio apartment that was connected to a larger main house and beautiful courtyard. I took one look at the ramshackle kitchen filled with primitive, outdated appliances and immediately felt disheartened. It took me a few days to even figure out how to turn on the gas stove!

On day three I announced, "Finally! I just got this old stove working. What does everyone want to eat?"

"Spaghetti!" Nathaniel shouted.

Gary put his arm around my waist. "Spaghetti sounds good to me."

Bethany didn't answer, so I walked over to the couch where she was reading. "Bethany?"

"Oh, yeah, whatever's fine," Bethany said as she was briefly summoned from Narnia.

"Wonderful! Spaghetti it is!" I said.

I burrowed through the misshapen tin pans and found what I needed for sauce and pasta. Despite my previous victory in getting the gas lit it would be a full hour before the low flame would bring water to a boil. My family was famished and endlessly begging for food.

Gary and Nathaniel had been killing time with a game of chess. Turning from the board Nathaniel said, "Mum, when will it be ready?"

"Bada-bing bada-boom, checkmate!" Gary said with a smirk on his face as he moved his marble Aztec warrior into the triumphant position.

"I can't win when I'm absolutely starving," Nathaniel whined.

"I keep reading the same paragraph over and over because I'm too hungry to think," Bethany added.

"Okay, come set the table then," I said, a little more grumpily than I intended. Hunger was getting to me, too. "It's almost ready."

Eventually we enjoyed our first home–cooked meal in Taxco. We put the leftovers in a container and set them in the ancient fridge.

The following day Nathaniel heated up a serving of spaghetti in an old, dented aluminum pan. When the spaghetti began to burn, I added some tap water.

"There, that'll help," I said.

"Thanks. It looks yummy."

Later that day Nathaniel complained of stomach cramps. Before we knew it, his cramps had progressed into projectile vomiting, severe diarrhea, and a high fever. It dawned on me that I'd made a huge mistake by adding tap water to his spaghetti.

Five days into our life in Mexico and Nathaniel had contracted typhoid fever!

Gary and I took the night watch while Bethany lay awake fearful for her brother's life.

Bethany turned over in her bed. "Mum, is he going to be okay?"

"Yes, honey. Go back to sleep." Little did I know that she had been awake all night.

Nathaniel was in grave danger. Right after Nathaniel was born, his newborn screening test had revealed a metabolic disorder in which the body's ability to process body fats is deficient. Frequently children with this deficiency collapse into a metabolic coma and die from any illness that produces a high fever, vomiting, or diarrhea.

Even when we lived in Colorado, anytime Nathaniel contracted a simple illness, it was scary. Now he had come down with typhoid fever while we were alone deep in the interior of southern Mexico.

"Honey, get me another bag." I said, as I tied up yet another plastic bag full of vomit.

"I can't find any more," Gary responded.

Bethany raised up and leaned on her elbow. "They're in the little cabinet in the kitchen. I put them there after we got home from the *mercado*."

As Gary left my side to get the bags, I started to cry and said, "Honey, he's burning up."

"Don't panic. He will be okay," Gary responded tersely as he tried to keep his own emotions in check. Bethany quietly began to pray as she heard me crying and listened to Nathaniel's moans and vomiting.

The morning sun brought respite to our weary emotions despite Nathaniel being consumed with fever. We talked to the resident caretakers, Oscar and Silvia, who would later become our cherished friends. Oscar told us he had a friend who was a physician. Fifteen minutes later, the doctor walked up the stone stairs to our little efficiency.

My mind was muddled with sleep deprivation and concern. Thankfulness filled my heart for my husband who had a stronger grasp of the Spanish language as well as a factual way of thinking in a crisis. The physician's kindhearted manner and protective nature comforted me. I was struck by the stark difference between his kindness and the severe risk of death and disease on the mission field. He prescribed strong antibiotics and a medicine to stop vomiting.

Gary left immediately for the pharmacy while Bethany and I continued to discard bags of vomit.

Nathaniel tended to see everything in tropical Mexico as though he were Bilbo Baggins being thrust into an adventure to climb mountains and slay dragons. For him, not even a life–threatening case of typhoid fever could dampen his youthful enthusiasm.

Within two days, he was feeling better. Within a week he was back to wanting to climb mountains and forge rivers.

Conversely, Bethany felt non-stop challenges and cultural adjustments. As an introvert, she struggled with being shoved into our very extroverted surroundings. The local children loved Bethany, and her blond hair and blue eyes amazed them. Still, she felt uncomfortable with their focused attention. She experienced social anxiety and wanted to respond in culturally appropriate ways, but many times none of us knew what that might be. We all made enormous blunders but, for Bethany, her perceived failures were especially painful to endure.

A few months after Nathaniel's brush with typhoid, we rented an apartment with high ceilings and concrete construction. It reminded us of a warehouse. Because of this, when Gary and I crawled into bed each night we felt as if we were sleeping in Costco rather than a warm and inviting home.

Our new neighbors, Carlos, Susana, and their toddler Camila, lived in the apartment directly above ours. They brought ice cream to welcome our family the day we moved in, but the following Saturday is when our friendship truly began.

Feeling cold from the early morning chill I snuggled up to my perpetually warm husband and said, "Honey, I would like to go into town today and get the mattresses for Nathaniel and Bethany."

"Hmmm, yeah, that would be fine," Gary responded still half asleep. "I also want to stop at the hardware store to see if they carry wood for my bookcases."

"If we go this morning the mattresses could be delivered before bedtime. The kids have been sleeping on the floor for nearly a week since we moved in."

Gary pulled me closer. "You know we still don't have a key for the balcony doors. If we all go into town, the doors will be unlocked."

Startled, I sat up. "I forgot about that. Someone could easily climb down from the balcony upstairs and walk right into this apartment."

"You're the one who met the neighbors while I was in town. What do you think about them?"

"I don't have a clue. Carlos and Susana seemed to be friendly, but I feel in a constant state of alert trying to figure everyone out."

Gary reached for his athletic shorts. "It should be fine. We won't be gone long."

"Yeah, right," I laughed. "Every single thing that we've attempted to do in this country has taken much longer than we thought it would."

We showered and prepared for the day. Gary locked the front door while Nathaniel and Bethany ran down to wait on the *combi* bus. I lingered and looked up at Carlos and Susana's apartment. I wondered if we were being wise to leave all our earthly possessions free for the taking.

Our destination was on the outskirts of town and required a *combi* change at the center of town, or *zocalo*. Soon we arrived at Aurrera, a crowded big–box store owned by Walmart. We quickly found where the mattresses were located. Our kids, who were bored with the decisions related to level of firmness and quality, chose what they wanted as quickly as possible. Gary left me with the mattresses and went to the front to pay and ask about delivery. He came back a few minutes later.

"They don't deliver," Gary stated.

"Did you already pay for them?"

"Yes, that's what I went to the checkout to do," Gary said, annoyed at the situation.

"What will we do? We don't even have a car let alone a truck."

"I know." Gary was frustrated at my habit of stating the obvious and expecting him to fix it.

I leaned on the stack of mattresses trying not to be as weary in body as I felt in soul. "Do you think Oscar and Silvia would know anyone who could help?"

The kids were tired of waiting. As Bethany fidgeted, Nathaniel said, "We'll meet you back here later, okay?" Both of them ran toward the Lego aisle before we could give an answer.

"Do you think Oscar would know anyone with a truck?" I repeated.

Gary felt the pressure mounting. "I don't know. Give me time to think."

"I'll be in the grocery section when you need me," I said walking away and feeling the sting of his tone.

Surrounded by unfamiliar products, I struggled to find a cereal box ingredient list that didn't include high-fructose corn syrup as the number-one ingredient.

At that moment, our new neighbor Carlos rounded the corner. "*Hola*, Rachel."

I was startled by his presence. "*¡O! ¡Hola*, Carlos!"

"*Cómo estás?*" he asked.

"*Ah, bien, bien,*" I stated without reference to the ensuing mattress disaster. "*Y tú?*"

"*Bien, bien,* good. Susana is looking at color for the hairs," he responded.

"Ahh, *sí, sí.*" I laughed at the weary expression on his face.

"Where is Gary?"

I explained that Gary was standing guard by the mattresses we had just purchased, but we had no idea how to get them home.

"Oh, Rachel, let me help to you. I have a friend with a truck. I will call to him."

"*Muchas gracias,* Carlos. That means so much to us," I said warmly to the wonderful neighbor Gary and I had previously suspected as a threat to the security of our home.

Susana came up beside Carlos. She was smiling broadly with red hair dye in her hand and two-year-old Camila by her side. "*Hola,*" she said shyly.

"*Hola,*" I responded with equal timidity.

Carlos had previously lived in Cabo San Lucas and knew English moderately well. Susana, on the other hand, understood very little English but what she didn't grasp in words she made up for in affection, kindness, and a goofy sense of humor.

Carlos spoke to his friend on the phone while I found Nathaniel and Bethany. We walked back to Gary and I explained that Carlos was going to help us.

"I am so relieved. I didn't know what to do," Gary said, slipping an arm around my waist. "Sometimes, in a different culture, everything is so difficult to figure out."

"I know." I smiled and returned his embrace. "I'm thankful Carlos saw me. I can't believe they are so happy to help us."

We waited in the parking garage of the Aurrera warehouse for several hours as Carlos's friend drove from an unknown but obviously distant location, probably via a local pub.

Building relationships and being generous with time and resources are values of the Mexican culture. Because of this, we didn't feel like we were imposing upon Carlos and Susana by accepting their kind offer.

Instead, it was the beginning of our hearts being knit together in the beauty of friendship with bonds as close and deep as family.

As we waited for the friend with the truck to arrive, Bethany played with Camila while Carlos shared with us the grief that he still felt from his mom's death two years prior. It surprised me that after two years he still grieved the loss of his mom. I had no idea at that moment, but this was a harbinger of the connection that we would later share because of the loss of a loved one.

Three hours later, Gary and Nathaniel went with the mattresses in the bumpy truck while Bethany and I rode with Carlos and Susana in their blue VW bug.

We drove down the dirt road toward home. As we pulled in front of our apartment, I looked up at our balcony doors. I thought of my earlier concern and the need I had felt for bolted and locked doors.

I knew my life would never be the same.

On that day my heart became one with the Mexican people. Because of the love extended to us I decided to stop being fearful of every unknown noise, person, or situation. My affection had been consummated while I leaned on a couple of cheap mattresses and allowed my heart to hear a Mexican man, who I had previously mistrusted, share devotion to his mom and how precious she had been to him.

I was forever altered and eternally grateful for that experience. Carlos and Susana became our very closest friends and compadres. We were family and shared each other's joys and challenges—even the most devastating event in my life that was yet to come.

Six months later, Gary and I got up early so we could surprise Carlos on his birthday by singing "*Las Mañanitas*" to him before he left for work.

I knocked on Nathaniel's door as I opened it, then gently jostled him. "Nathaniel, wake up. It's time to sing for Carlos."

"Aww, Mum, what time is it? I don't want to get up."

"It's close to 6:00. He's in the shower by 6:15, so we've got to do it now."

There were ventilation window shafts that opened within Nathaniel's bathroom. Because they were concrete, they echoed up and down between the apartments and the rooftop where they opened. These window shafts carried every sound. That's how we knew when Carlos showered every morning—and how we planned on delivering our surprise birthday song.

I walked across the hall. "Bethany, honey, wake up. It's time to sing to Carlos."

She moaned and pulled the covers over her head.

I shuffled into the kitchen and warmed up a cup of coffee from yesterday's pot. Gary came in and kissed me passionately.

"Honey, the kids are getting up," I said.

"Yeah, well, they're not here now." He pulled me tightly to himself.

I smiled playfully and reluctantly disengaged from this pleasurable moment with my husband.

The kids, Gary, and I gathered in Nathaniel's bathroom with joyful abandon. We sang loudly, knowing our voices would carry perfectly to Carlos and Susana's bathroom above us.

"Estas son las mañanitas
Que cantaba el rey David
Hoy por ser día de tu santo
Te las cantamos a ti. . ."

By the second verse Carlos was laughing and shouting down at us, *"Gracias mis amigos, gracias."*

"¡Feliz cumpleaños!" We shouted as everyone broke into laughter.

Later that evening we would celebrate with *postre*, songs, and games, but for now we were content knowing that this early morning revelry had given our dear friend happiness on his birthday.

Two

THE SHADOW OF GRIEF

"If we are going to wait until every possible hindrance has been removed before we do a work for the Lord, we will never attempt to do anything."

T.J. Bach, Missionary to Venezuela

The residence we shared with Carlos and Susana in the *barrio de Casallas* was down a dirt road from a soccer field where wild horses grazed and children played after school.

Directly south from the stark three–story apartment sat an old, abandoned brick building. Its gorgeous architecture and the surrounding natural growth of trees and flowers seemed to beckon us.

Soon we began to entertain the crazy idea of it becoming our ministry outreach center and family home. Every time we walked past the building, Gary's pace would slow as he imagined our neighbors coming through the wide–open iron doors for Bible studies, outreach fiestas, and Saturday afternoon tacos. I was reticent because I had no idea what dangers lurked behind the broken glass, graffiti, and the dense foliage filled with who-knew-what kinds of creatures.

What my husband lacked in youthful years, he more than made up for in passion and vision. One day as we wandered down the rocky dirt road, Gary grabbed my hand with excitement. "Let's go inside."

The deserted structure was protected by years of thick jungle overgrowth and a spider hanging in front of the gate who we less than affectionately referred to as "the guard spider."

As Gary dragged me forward, I shouted, "Honey, the giant spider is right in front of me!"

"It's okay, just go around him."

I yanked back on his hand. "If you'd stop pulling me so fast, I could do that!"

Back home in Colorado, panic would grip me if any type of critter became lodged in my thick curly hair. The mountains of tropical Mexico took this fear to new heights.

Slowly I maneuvered around the enormous arachnid and climbed through the tangled underbrush.

We came to the large iron doors with their broken windows. Gary reached through the jagged glass, untwisted the heavy wire clamp, and opened the door.

Adrenaline surged through our bodies.

"What if someone is in there?" I asked nervously.

Gary put his finger to his lips. "Let's walk through quietly."

The possibility of finding a building for ministry filled us with excitement. At the same time, we also felt terror at what we might find lurking behind the walls of this abandoned structure in the drug cartel–infested mountains of southern Mexico.

Even without fully knowing the local laws, we were pretty sure that breaking and entering was a criminal offense. My vivid imagination raced with images of distant isolated dungeons. Instinctively, I knew that a Mexican prison is not a preferred destination on anyone's bucket list.

Thankfully, machine guns did not greet us. Instead, we found sewer rats, graffiti, animal skeletons, and the evidence of all types of sexual activity that had taken place in hidden corners.

"What was that?" I whispered

"You just stepped on a mouse. I saw him run in front of you."

I shook my foot and ran away from the smashed mouse. "Ew, that's disgusting. He crunched!"

Gary gestured toward a nearby rat carcass. "Thankfully, it wasn't anything larger."

Looking around, we processed our surroundings. Several inches of accumulated dirt covered a beautiful red tile floor in the main living area. The stunning design and character of the brick and stone walls felt warm and alluring compared to the concrete of our apartment. The sun shone through several large arched doorways with forged iron that framed the glass.

We stood in quiet reverence.

Gary's voice cracked with pent–up emotion. "This is an incredible ministry center! We could get a bunch of people in here for Bible studies and outreach events. And we could live upstairs."

"Maybe." I curled my tense fingers around his strong hand. "Let's go see what's up there."

Many sunny windows brightened the stone stairway yet mounds of filth darkened it. Around every corner in the upper level we saw beauty as well as every vile device imaginable. We stepped over an accumulation of rat droppings but later surmised them to be the resident coatimundi's frequented pit stop. We climbed over broken bottles, used condoms, and sewer rat skeletons.

"All we've been able to find is one bedroom," I observed. "I can't imagine how to make that work for Nathaniel and Bethany."

"I know," Gary responded with disappointment.

THE SHADOW OF GRIEF

We didn't want to entertain the idea that despite the stunning brick and stone construction, this building might not be a realistic option for our family. We nervously walked around each corner. When our exploration gave us confidence that we wouldn't experience a horror story at the hands of armed drug cartels, Gary said, "Let's go get the kids."

We ran up the road to our apartment and called out to Nathaniel and Bethany for them to come join us in the adventure.

"You broke into the old building?" Nathaniel asked as he looked with boyish admiration at his dad.

"Yeah, we did," I answered. "You gotta come see. It's amazing!"

Bethany twirled through the living room as if in another world. She bumped into her daddy.

"You'll want to change out of that dress into some jeans and hiking shoes," Gary told her. "There's a lot of filth and broken glass over there."

Grabbing his tape measure and mag light, Gary prepared for another adventure down the hill.

Meanwhile, I shook off imaginary spiders from my clothes and changed my blouse just in case an eight–legged hitchhiker had gotten lodged in a location where I did not desire him to be.

The four of us dashed down the hill back to the foreboding building that held so much potential and an equal amount of danger.

Our children could not imagine anything more exciting than exploring this abandoned building with its hidden rooms and surrounding tropical jungle.

As we explored, we discovered that the house consisted of four tiers that were built into the mountain.

In the lowest level, we found ourselves walking on broken glass and bumping into discarded display cases used in the silver industry.

We climbed the iron spiral stairs to the Spanish–inspired *cocina*. I tried to look past the rat skeletons and filth covering every inch of the Telvera tile to appreciate the intricate beauty of this Mexican kitchen.

Enormous arched iron windows looked out over the nearby mountains. In fact, arched windows offered sweeping views throughout the entire main level including the kitchen, breakfast room, dining room, living room, and office.

We dodged dead animals, fecal material, and broken glass with every step. But our family did not focus on these things. In our imagination we removed all the filth with a click of a mental button and envisioned the ministry potential as well the beauty in the baroque artistry that surrounded us.

Adjacent to the iron front door where we had first entered, multi-hued stone stairs led to the master bedroom, laundry area, and a long room complete with a wooden stage defaced with violent graffiti and littered broken beer bottles.

Two tower rooms flanked the ends of the tiered tile roof. From our perspective below they seemed to be cramped forts with high turreted ceilings built onto the ends of the roof. We followed Gary's direction and scrambled up the spiral stairs to one of the towers. Mold–covered walls greeted us, along with an area that contained plenty of space for teen hideaways.

Gary got out his tape measure and said, "Here, hold this end."

Both rooms were situated on either end of the house and measured a comfortable 10x10. All four of us looked at each other in amazement and knew that the towers would be perfect bedrooms for Nathaniel and Bethany.

The risky enterprise of this house bade us onward, and we knew this ominous structure was destined to be our home. Intense prayer and a passion for outreach guided us over the next many months. We rented the abandoned structure from a local silversmith and began the process of transforming it into a beautiful and functioning home and ministry center.

Once again, God used the circumstances of our lives to endear us to the local community. The little neighborhood *combi* bus, driven by our dear friend Beto, stopped and gave the locals impromptu tours of the restoration project on the infamous "very bad house." The things that had previously occurred within the walls of our new home terrified our neighbors. We heard legends that we couldn't fully comprehend because of our limited Spanish.

We only knew the inward passions that drove us, which worked to captivate the hearts of the local people. We had open doors into their hearts that would not have been possible otherwise.

Even so, the renovation project proved to be more difficult than any of us had imagined.

Early in our marriage Gary and I had restored an 1890s farmhouse in Pennsylvania; therefore, we approached this enterprise with smug confidence. *This isn't our first rodeo*, we reasoned.

We did not realize a shadow had fallen on our lives, a shadow I would not fully understand for ten more months.

At the time, Gary and I both felt an urgency to complete the project as soon as we possibly could. This meant weeks and months of grueling, nearly non-stop struggles, many of which could not have been put on hold even if we had wanted to take a break.

God did not caution us to slow down or stop working. I cannot lament the decisions we made that flowed from our passion for ministry and our obedience to how the Lord was leading us.

One of the more dangerous and crippling obstacles we faced happened after we left our apartment and moved into the partially renovated house.

We'd lived there for several weeks when one day we discovered raw sewage seeping through the walls in the lower level.

We had no idea what was transpiring in the hidden recesses of the building. All we knew was that it was getting worse. Within a few days, raw sewage was seeping out of every wall of our home and spilling onto the floors.

I poured gallons of bleach into the toilets so that the disinfectant would flow through the walls along with the fecal matter. The smell was atrocious, and we could not have felt more discouraged.

Gary worked relentlessly along with the men of the neighborhood to obtain the necessary paperwork to give us permission to repair the public sewer line outside of our home. After a full month the documents cleared the Mexican Department of Health.

A gang of local guys worked as quickly as possible to rescue our family from the odoriferous and deadly abyss in which we were living.

One afternoon, long after the raw sewage had been thoroughly cleaned, our dear friend and *combi* driver Beto walked up the dirt road and greeted Gary and me as we were clearing brush around the grounds with a machete.

"Gary, we would like you and your family to come eat with us," Beto said in Spanish.

We had never been invited to Beto's home before. Gary put down his machete. "We would be honored. What day would you like us to come?"

"*Comida* is in an hour and we will be waiting for you in our home," Beto said warmly.

"*Sí, sí, muchas gracias*, Beto," I said, all the while ignoring the internal panic of not having time to prepare.

Beto and Gary chatted for a few minutes while I grabbed Nathaniel and Bethany and flew to the house toward the kitchen. We could not go to our dear friend's home empty handed and I had nothing prepared in my pantry.

Impatiently, I said, "Bethany, what ingredients do we have?"

"I don't know, I think we used the last of the chocolate when we made cookies for Oscar and Silvia."

"Nathaniel, turn the oven on medium."

He saluted. "Ma'am! Yes, ma'am!" he said, mocking my barked orders.

Twirling in a whimsical dance, Bethany made her way to the pantry shelves. "We have oatmeal but not much flour."

"Then oatmeal it will have to be," I responded.

When the cookies came out of the oven, to my chef's eyes they appeared ordinary and uninviting. "I don't like how they look."

Nathaniel grabbed a hot pad and pulled the last tray out of the oven. "Mum, they're fine."

I picked up a cookie then tossed it back onto the baking sheet. "I don't like how brown they are."

"Mum, they're oatmeal cookies, they're yummy," Bethany said as she licked a batter–filled spoon.

I felt helpless and stressed because of the last–minute invitation. I wanted everything to be perfect, but perfection was proving to be elusive.

"Let's make some frosting," I suggested. "It won't take much time."

"Mum, that's not necessary," Nathaniel moaned.

"Well, I feel they need something to make them more appetizing."

Bethany picked up a mixing bowl and said, "Fine!"

We quickly made vanilla frosting, trying to transform plain and ordinary oatmeal into something special.

Only an hour after being invited, Gary, Nathaniel, Bethany, and I walked down the hill to the poorer section of our *barrio*. We were apprehensive, not knowing what this afternoon meal would require in knowledge of Spanish and awareness of culture.

Beto greeted us while his more reserved wife and young children stood by timidly. Several generations of family were represented and as many white plastic chairs inside as out. Dogs and chickens roamed freely between the exterior and interior of the home. Beto excitedly showed Gary his audio equipment which provided the entire neighborhood with a constant source of twangy ranchero music.

The children's grandma or *abuelita* served delicious tamales with a complex red sauce that I have never been able to duplicate in my kitchen. While we were being seated, I handed the plate of cookies to Beto's wife, Augustina, and with visible anxiety she passed them to her nieces and nephews who were Nathaniel and Bethany's ages.

"*Uh, no, gracias,*" one of the nieces said as she shyly passed the plate to her siblings.

We watched in surprise as the children regarded a simple oatmeal cookie in disdain, afraid that it would be some disgusting foreign food.

Augustina shot a disapproving look at her niece. At that moment I realized Augustina and I felt a mutual fear of offending each other. Knowing that we shared the same struggles to overcome cultural puzzles with no picture to guide us helped me to relax in various situations involving our dear Mexican friends and neighbors

The oatmeal cookies, which I had previously feared were too ordinary, ended up being exotically peculiar to our friends. The younger kids bravely attempted a taste, but the teenagers outright refused. To their eyes, the frosting looked like mayonnaise and they could not imagine such a *combi*nation "*para el postre*," or for dessert.

Being welcomed into this local family was an important step into our good standing within the *barrio*. And despite the mutual nervousness and foreign ways, our individual families understood each other's hearts, and by that we were drawn together.

This joyous occasion worked toward the good that God wanted us to do in this remote area of Mexico. The love that we shared crossed the barriers of language and culture.

In Romans we read, "And we know that in all things God works for the good of those who love him, who have been called according to his purpose" (Romans 8:28).

Typically, this verse is only extracted from Scripture when we hope to find comfort in a tragedy. But God can bring good into all situations, even wonderfully adventurous things that we only see as one dimensional. He can bring a mosaic of good out of all circumstances into which he leads us. Gary and I knew that God had led us into this renovation project in remote southern Mexico. At the time, the only thing that we could see was the outcome of the finished structure. But along way, God used our journey to bind our lives to the locals in a very deep way.

We did not know that disaster would befall our family, and how much we would need the depth of these relationships in the coming months. Our neighbors had a respect and affection for us that would have taken many years to develop had we lived an unnoticed life in the *barrio de Casallas*.

The old abandoned house, like Mexico herself, represented a dichotomy between sinister and innocent, mangled and beautiful.

Three

THE TRAGEDY OF GRIEF

*"May I burn up for thee, consume my life, my God,
for it is thine. I seek not a long life, but a full one
like Yours, Lord Jesus."*

Jim Elliot

It was July on the mission field in the tropical mountains where we lived. Without a Rocky Mountain blizzard or summer hailstorm, one season in Mexico flows into the next with relative ease.

In the States, the arrival of mid-summer gardens, camping trips, and fireworks were always fun reminders that Gary's birthday was around the corner, and it would be time to celebrate all that he meant to us.

In Mexico, the familiarity of Colorado was missing. There were, however, constant reminders and reasons to celebrate my selfless husband, such as his tireless leadership, protection, and care for us during the long months of physical labor on our ministry center and home.

During the exhausting final days of our renovation project, Nathaniel, Bethany, and I had planned a surprise birthday party to honor Gary. I also had made reservations for the two of us at a romantic B&B where I prepared to lavish my husband with passion and admiration.

One week before the big day, I walked to the bottom of the spiral stairs that twisted up to Nathaniel's tower bedroom. "Do you have the wrapping paper? I've looked everywhere for it."

"Oops, yeah, I do."

"Can I come up and get it?"

"Sure."

I didn't dislike going up and down the spiral stairs to the tower rooms as much as Gary did. My five-foot-two stature mirrored the smaller Latino frame that the stairs had been designed to accommodate. Occasionally, however, my fear of heights kicked in when winding my way back down.

The monsoons, along with years of lawlessness, had created putrid odors and exploding mold in Nathaniel and Bethany's bedrooms. Before painting Nathaniel's room a lively blue, we had drenched the brick walls with bleach to kill any contaminant that had been entombed from the years of depravity. Nathaniel's resulting sunny *azul* walls reassured my soul and soothed my concerns.

As I finished looping up the twisted stairs, I could see into Nathaniel's room and saw Bethany sitting on the floor surrounded by markers, tape, and glitter.

"What are you guys doing?" I asked.

Nathaniel looked up from his desk where he was playing with Legos, an abandoned poster for his dad nearby. He sighed. "Trying to figure out what to write on Dad's poster. And where in the world I'm going to hide it when I'm done."

Pushing aside wrapping paper, tape, and scissors I sat down on Nathaniel's bed. "I know what you mean. With all the renovations, there's no place to hide anything. I was trying to sneak his birthday presents into our room when I discovered him in there building screens for our windows. It's such a pain to try to surprise him while we're finishing the house."

Nathaniel popped the burgundy Lego piece into his favorite Victorian building. "You're telling me. When we were at the hardware store, he asked why I wanted to run over to the lady selling candy. Of course, he didn't know I was buying it for him."

"That's good." I laughed, "It was easier when you guys were little, and he knew what you were doing so that he could play along."

"And give us extra money to buy his presents!" Bethany said as she held up her poster.

"Oh, I like that, honey, it's really pretty. Dad will love the ice cream stickers. Where did you get those?"

"I brought them from Colorado. I always put them on Dad's cards."

Nathaniel grabbed his poster and had a sudden idea. "Oh, Mum, it was so funny. Carlos asked me what gifts Dad enjoyed for his birthday and I said chocolate. He looked at me so strange. I laughed and tried to explain but I don't think he got it."

I laughed with a snort, and my coffee spilled on my shirt. "That's hilarious, I don't think many local men get chocolate from their *compadres* for their birthday." Still laughing I said, "In Mexico tequila would more likely be a manly gift than foil-wrapped chocolates. Well, I better get downstairs while Dad has gone into town. Are you guys finished with the wrapping paper?"

"I am, but Nathaniel isn't," Bethany responded and handed the garish sheets to me.

"It's okay, I'll come get it when I'm ready," Nathaniel said. "Right now, I have a great idea for Dad's poster!"

I stood up trying to figure out how to carry the rolls of wrapping paper, tape, and scissors down the spiral stairs and not spill any more coffee onto my blouse. "I'm glad you have birthday ideas now that you have stopped building Legos."

"Yeah, yeah, but it helped me to think."

Bethany, trying to protect her brother's honor said, "Mum, it really does help him get ideas."

"I know, its fine," I said with adoration of my son's creativity. "Although we do have a lot of work yet to do, and it's only a week before Dad's birthday."

"We know, Mum, we know," they assured me as I wound my way down the stairs.

Throughout the following days I heard giggles and whispers in the secret corners of the Moore household as Nathaniel and Bethany tucked presents and posters out of sight.

Gary and I felt the heavy responsibility of the house renovation, therefore, we couldn't be as lighthearted as our children. In addition, we were exhausted. Five days before Gary's birthday, tempers had flared, and harsh words had been exchanged between us.

Several hours later, Gary was standing on the ladder installing framed screens into our bedroom windows. He had planned on making screens for each of the seventy-two windows throughout the house to keep the coatimundis and mosquitos outside where they belonged.

I put my hand gently on his arm and said, "Honey, let's go into town this afternoon, just the two of us, for *comida*."

"That sounds good. Where do you want to eat?" he said.

Tears welled up in my eyes. "I think if we sat quietly at Adobe it would be relaxing. . . and romantic. I'm sorry about this morning."

Gary banged the last corner of the frame in place, put his hammer in his tool belt, and climbed down the ladder. "I'm sorry too. I will be glad when we're finished with this damn project," he said as he put his arm around me in desperation.

"We're almost done, honey. You've worked so hard and accomplished an incredible amount on this house. We'll be able to finally relax and begin to enjoy life," I said as I kissed him gently.

"I know, I'm just so tired. I've never been this exhausted and I don't know why."

I felt an ominous foreboding at how often he commented on how frazzled and worn out he felt. I rationalized away my fears, reminding myself that it would have been abnormal to not be exhausted during a project of this magnitude. I longed for the day when we would be finished.

"What time do you want to head into town?" Gary asked.

"Let's catch the *combi* around 2:00 and then we can walk around a bit before we eat. I'd like to show you the store on the corner where I saw the pretty ceramic jewelry case."

With passion in his eyes Gary grabbed me and I pulled away. "Honey, you've been working all morning and you have the sweat to prove it. But if you wear your tweed jacket into town. . ." I said as I smiled teasingly.

"Hmm. I'll finish the other window and then I'll get a shower."

I brushed my hand over the back of his neck. "I'll be thinking about you."

"What about?"

"Never mind, you'll find out," I said provocatively as I walked away.

I wanted to keep the mystery alive, so I quickly mentioned to the kids that Dad and I had to go into town without giving an explanation. They barely looked up from their current birthday project.

At 2:00 I was running down the driveway in my sexy low–cut dress. Gary and I met up at the iron gate that I had painted a deep green. Gary looked handsome in his tweed jacket and I felt pretty and playful.

The women of Taxco had influenced me, and I had long since ditched my Colorado hikers for more feminine high heels. I enjoyed the cultural change and it never seemed like an awkward adaptation. Despite my blond hair and hazel eyes, in my heart I felt Latina. Everything about the local women resonated in my soul, and it was very natural for me to flow within the feminine allure that typified the Mexican woman.

We strolled through Taxco and then walked from the center of town on *Cuauhtémoc* to the *Restaurante el Adobe*. The waiters knew our family and gave Gary and me our favorite romantic spot on a small balcony that overlooked the city. We leaned in toward each other and talked quietly, enjoying the intimacy that we both cherished.

We rode the *combi* back to the big old house as the tropical sun was setting and felt renewed in body and spirit.

Gary opened the iron front door. We walked into the living room and saw Nathaniel reading on the overstuffed chair. Bethany, immersed in her own book, was curled up on the couch.

"Do you guys wanna watch a movie tonight?" I asked.

Nathaniel, looking up from a conversation between Watson and Holmes said, "Sure, that would be fun."

Bethany agreed.

"Dad and I had a relaxing afternoon and thought it would be fun if we made some popcorn and watched *The Egg and I*. I don't think you guys ever saw it."

"Never heard of it," Nathaniel said.

"I thought it would be fun to watch since it's about a couple who buys an old house and has one crazy adventure after another fixing it up."

"Oh, boy, that sounds familiar," Bethany said, finally interested enough to leave Meg, Jo, and Laurie.

"Okay, who wants popcorn?" I asked.

Gary laughed. "That's a silly question."

"We all do!" Bethany and Nathaniel shouted.

"Bethany, we'll make popcorn while the guys get the movie set up."

Gary and Nathaniel plopped their feet on the empty coffee table and with commanding manly tones said, "We're ready! Bring on the popcorn."

"Ha! The laptop needs to be brought in and the movie rented on Amazon."

"Yeah, yeah, it's always something," Gary teased as I walked past him on my way to the kitchen.

We enjoyed an evening bursting with laughter as we empathized with the mishaps of Fred MacMurray and Claudette Colbert portrayed in black and white on the screen.

The next morning, as the scavenging roosters began to crow, we dragged ourselves out of bed.

It was four days before Gary's surprise birthday celebration and the very last day of the renovation project.

After the plague of the raw sewage, I was militant in my orders to disinfect our home. Because of this, Nathaniel and Bethany had mop, bucket, and bleach in hand as they embarked on a final cleaning mission in the downstairs level.

Gary went into town to purchase the glass he would need to finish repairing the broken windows throughout the house.

After returning from town in a taxi, Gary placed extra pesos in the driver's hand. Then he headed up the driveway toward the house carrying two panes of heavy glass. He put the glass safely in his office, then came back outside to wait on a *combi* to catch a ride back into town for the final two panes.

This last errand would signify the concluding chapter of the many tormented months of struggle and trials. The finish line to this enormous renovation project was finally within sight.

While he waited for the *combi*, I joined him. We sat together on the front stairs, our gaze lingering on the purple bougainvillea that framed the green iron gate, and I smiled at the memory of yesterday's romantic getaway. As it did every day, the strong sweet smell of the surrounding guavas wafted through the air.

The monsoons had produced abundant tropical flowers, songbirds, and foliage, and we watched the motmot bird and enjoyed the quiet respite of our time together.

Part of me wanted to tell Gary about the surprise that we had planned for his birthday because I knew it would encourage him and help to lift the heavy burden that he had been carrying. But I knew I couldn't. Nathaniel, Bethany, and I had sworn each other to secrecy, and none of us would break our vow of silence.

Gary looked at me with affection and quietly said, "I love you. . . "

Abruptly, he cried out in an alarming tone, "Oh, wow!" Then my strong husband hit the pavement.

"Nathaniel! Bethany!" I screamed in terror.

Gary was face down on the concrete. He was unconscious but writhing and moaning. I tried to turn him over so that he could breathe, but his six-foot frame was too much for me. "Oh, Jesus, oh, Jesus help me!" I prayed.

Nathaniel and Bethany came lunging up the iron spiral stairs from the lower level, panic already in their faces.

And then they saw their father on the ground.

"Mum, move over!" Nathaniel commanded as he rolled his dad's body over and started giving him CPR.

Breathe in, blow out, rest, rest.

"Jesus, Jesus, help us," I continued to cry as I lay on the pavement holding my husband's hand.

Chest compression, breath in, blow out, rest.

Bethany was still standing in shock in the front doorway.

"Call Carlos and Susana!" I yelled to her. "Tell them to come quickly!"

Bethany stumbled up the stone stairs to the phone in her daddy's office. "Carlos, I think Dad just had a heart attack!"

"Oh, God no! We will be right there!" Carlos said.

Bethany staggered back down the stairs and stood in the doorway watching her family unravel.

In subsequent years, the three of us would attempt to fix our family and go back to the way things had been. But I believe at that moment, as the breath in Gary's lungs disappeared, deep in our hearts we knew we were not only witnessing the death of a husband and father, but the complete annihilation of our family.

The *combi* pulled up and the driver, our friend Don Luis, opened the driver's side door and ran through the gate and toward our house.

"What can I do?" he asked in Spanish.

Nathaniel ordered between breaths, "Call an ambulance!"

Combi passengers disembarked and stood in our driveway, as other caring and curious neighbors walked up the cobbles of our driveway.

Nathaniel continued CPR meticulously and with determination.

"Let me take over," someone offered in Spanish.

"No! Let me be!" Nathaniel commanded.

There are no words to describe what it feels like to watch your previously impish and fun–loving fifteen-year-old son clamp his mouth on his daddy's lips and attempt to breathe life into a dead man's lungs.

Bethany stood in the doorway and watched the scene as if it were a horrible movie being portrayed on a large hazy distant screen. There is no language to describe the trauma of a teenaged girl looking on as her strong manly father lay crumpled on the pavement.

Everything happened so quickly yet was in slow agonizing motion as normal life ceased to exist and trauma and loss began its ravaging and decaying effects upon our family.

I felt numb as I held the hand of the man with whom I had shared every intimacy.

"Jesus, Jesus! Please help us!" was my desperate and limited prayer.

The sounds that my husband made as he was dying is something I will never forget. To this day I cannot bear the faintest hint of a male groan and need to remove myself from any situation that reminds me of the trauma of that day.

Gary lost bladder control and I knew that was a sign of death. I also felt his left arm quiver from top to bottom as if his heart had made one last effort at life.

I was totally removed from the reality of the moment. In my head I knew what had happened, yet I was an observer from a very distant foggy place. Part of me knew that he had died, and yet I continued to desperately cling to the hope of life.

Carlos and Susana tried to comfort me. The *combi* bus remained stopped in front of our home—a symbol of something gone horribly wrong in our quiet little *barrio* where drivers never broke their routine or schedule.

The ambulance finally made its way down the rutted dirt road past the pigs, wandering chickens, and stray dogs. It was the same road on which Gary and I had frequently walked hand in hand and prayed for our friends and neighbors.

As Carlos ushered me into the house, I looked back and saw the defeated expression on the face of the EMT as he knelt by Gary's body.

I mumbled to Carlos, "Is he gone?"

Carlos responded with deep emotion and in a croaky voice said, "Yes, Rachel, he is."

Thirst filled my body. In shock, I felt strangely annoyed at our dear friends that no one would give me water. They surrounded me and sat me down, keeping me steady as someone stuck some strong–smelling stuff under my nose so that I wouldn't faint. But all I could think about was water.

"I need water, please," I cried out in Spanish.

"No! Very bad," a voice answered. (Someone later explained that water could have made me vomit which would have been life-threatening had I fainted.)

I had no awareness of my children at the time. I felt lightheaded and my emotions swam into murkiness.

The EMTs carried Gary's body past me and dropped him on the couch across from the chair where I was sitting. Plop! They treated his body if he were a sack of supplies from the local hardware store or a heavy bag of cement.

Everything felt hazy and as if I were detached from my body.

Eventually our friends and neighbors permitted me to sip on some water as *federales* carrying machine guns filled our home.

The police with their giant Uzi machine guns asked how my husband had died and what I had done to him while we were alone on the stairs.

Thankfully, Carlos translated because my ability to communicate in another language completely vanished. Later I realized that these were serious questions coming from the Mexican police where Napoleonic law dictates that a person is guilty until proven innocent. I had no understanding of the gravity of their questions nor of my nearly incoherent responses.

As I stared at my dead husband's body only a few feet away from me, an official—perhaps the equivalent of a coroner in the United States—demanded that we bury Gary immediately.

If I agreed, I knew my children and I would be required to participate in a funeral march to the town's hillside gravesite. But how could I make this journey only minutes after my husband's death? How could I possibly bury him when I couldn't even comprehend that he was dead?

We had witnessed locals on this pilgrimage before, sobbing as they carried a beloved family member in a box on their shoulders. I later found out they don't embalm bodies in Taxco, thus the pressure to bury their dead immediately.

Nathaniel in despair begged, "Can't we have more time? Can't we please have more time?"

I took my children out of the room and walked them methodically up the stairs to the more private area of our home. We sat down on the red tile floor in our laundry room, where Gary had recently added electricity, and I began to pray.

"God help us, we don't know what to do. Show us what to do," I prayed in desperation.

I knew we did not have the emotional or physical strength to bury him before the sun set that evening. Suddenly the thought came to my mind of cremation.

"Would you both be okay if Dad were cremated? I don't know if they even do that here, but that might be an answer."

"That's fine," Nathaniel responded in a daze.

"Whatever is okay," Bethany said.

"Are you both sure?"

Nathaniel stood up and in a detached state of shock said, "Yes, Mum, whatever."

With dread we slowly walked down the stairs.

Carlos put his arm around me.

I turned to him and asked, "Do you know the English word cremation?"

"*Ahhh, sí, sí.*"

"We don't know what to do but thought maybe we could have him cremated."

"Let me speak to them and I will tell to you."

"*Gracias,* Carlos."

Anyone who believes that the Latin American cultures are slow and easygoing has never had a loved one die within the borders of a

Spanish–speaking country. On the afternoon of my husband's death, the unmerciful law of the Mexican government required us to make rapid–fire judgments regarding life altering decisions.

Within twenty minutes, Carlos told me that officials from a crematorium in the neighboring city of Iguala would be at our home within the hour. Gary would be cremated in the morning, and we were to pick up his ashes at noon.

The officials instructed us to go to the kitchen as someone needed to examine Gary while he lay on the couch, and they did not want us to be present.

When Bethany, Nathaniel, and I were ushered back into the living room, Carlos gently told us it was time for us to say goodbye.

We knelt by his body. I felt no emotion as shock, confusion, and trauma took over my entire being.

I took Gary's hand, and was startled by how cold it was. I had anticipated his skin not feeling warm with life, but his gentle fingers were icy–cold with death. I mumbled some sentiments that I thought those around me expected to hear—but I felt too numb to even know what I was saying.

The three of us went through the rituals of the culture in which we were living. I felt locked into a foreign way of doing things despite the numbness and shock. Nothing we experienced remotely resembled the customs surrounding a death in the States, which of course added to the aspect of trauma that plundered our lives.

When the crematorium truck arrived, Carlos took off Gary's wedding ring and pulled his wallet from his pants and gave them to me. I was annoyed. *How could he do that? Why would he take my husband's wedding ring off his finger? And please leave his wallet alone.* It was abhorrent to me that Carlos was reaching into my husband's pants pocket.

At the time I didn't realize the bizarre nature of my thinking. My mind went to strange places. I remember thinking that I had always liked the shirt that Gary had on that morning—and I didn't want it to be burned up because then he could never wear it again. I said nothing as these nonsensical thoughts flooded my mind.

The men took a sheet from our bedroom, wrapped Gary's body in it, and carried him out to a vehicle. I felt annoyed that one of my bed sheets would be burned up. My brain seemed to be functioning at a strange sublevel of reality.

As the vehicle drove off with my husband's body, Carlos told me that we needed to go into Taxco to sign legal papers. Meanwhile, no one in the States even knew that Gary had died. None of his family knew anything had happened. I hadn't had even a moment to call anyone. Everything had transpired at an accelerated pace—and still was.

Carlos marched us from one official building to another, signing papers and explaining what had happened.

Carlos, Susana, and their two little children were with us for the duration of this horrid process. Their love and support were tremendous, but all I felt was shock and numbness.

Susana and I held each other while tears cascaded down our cheeks. We felt bonded together in love, our hearts and cultures further melded through this tragedy.

I looked up at Carlos as I signed yet another document at the county official's desk. I thought of our first conversation with him at the department store on the day we bought our mattresses, when he shared about his mother's death.

"Carlos." I stopped signing papers long enough to look up at him. "Gary is with your mom."

Carlos grabbed my hands and began to cry. "Oh, Rachel. . ." he said as he sobbed over yet another loss in his life.

It was late in the evening when we got back to our home. Nathaniel and Bethany rushed in the front door, no doubt heading to their hidden tower rooms in the labyrinth of our house.

I lingered and looked at the stairs where Gary and I had been sitting only a few hours before. My exhausted mind couldn't take it in. I tried to figure out how to walk over the place where he had died.

The location of his death felt both sacred and repulsive to me.

Was it a holy place? Or a location of unspeakable horror and dread?

In time, I came to understand that both were true and not mutually exclusive of each other.

Once inside our home, I remembered the birthday party. I thought of the gifts, cards, and posters that he would never see. I thought of the B&B where Gary and I would have had our own intimate celebration, just four days from now. How do you call and cancel reservations for a romantic getaway because your husband has died?

Carlos walked me into our living room. I looked at the couch where Gary's body had lain, and there were secretions on the dark green fabric.

"Oh, Carlos," I said, nearly collapsing, "Look at the mess on the couch. Could you help me clean it?"

"Yes, Rachel, I will help you. Whatever you need I will do for you."

I had no idea what had come out of Gary's body, but I couldn't bear to clean it alone. I filled a bucket with soap and water. My beloved Mexican friend and I knelt together and scrubbed the location where my dead husband's body had lain a few hours previous.

That night I placed a phone call to a dear friend in Colorado. She was not home at the time, so I blurted out to her husband that Gary had died.

I'll never forget his response.

"Well, that's not good."

I'm sure he had no idea how to respond to a dazed missionary calling from Mexico late at night to report the death of her husband.

But I remember in my bewildered thinking "not good" applied more to losing a favorite book or possibly the family pet.

It didn't seem to describe the horrific tragedy that had unraveled our lives.

Four

THE DARKNESS OF GRIEF

"The world changed to gray and emptiness, and Conor knew exactly where he was, exactly what the world had changed into. He was inside the nightmare."

Patrick Ness

*G**ary! I need to talk to you about what's happened!*

Strange thoughts kept reverberating through my mind. *How can I go through such a disaster and not tell Gary about it?*

I felt the need to call him back from the dead for a few minutes so that I could share the awful news with him.

Oh, honey, guess what just happened, you died! The deepest longing of my heart that first evening was a need to share with my husband the calamity that had befallen us.

The kids stayed with me in my room. Bethany slept in my bed and Nathaniel crashed on the floor.

"Honey, where's your hand?" I spoke in my sleep. "Where are you?"

"Mum, go back to sleep," Bethany whispered as I grasped for Gary's hand and found my daughter's small feminine one instead.

After a fitful night of sleep, I tried to make sense out of the queasy feeling in my stomach. The early morning sun rose above the mountains and brought unwanted definition to the forms around me. I saw Bethany sleeping on Gary's side of our bed and Nathaniel's rumpled blankets on the floor.

The distant sound of roosters crowing suggested comfort and familiarity, but comfort and familiarity disappeared as nightmares became reality.

On the surface, everything seemed as it always did. Street dogs roused themselves and gathered below our balcony hoping for a generous breakfast from my abundant kitchen. The tortilla man drove wildly on his scooter bringing the morning's first tortillas to each small concrete house along the rutted dirt road. Beto, driving the *combi* on his early morning route, had a cup of coffee in one hand and the steering wheel in the other. He made his first round past our house as he headed into town.

The tropical birds sang a sweet melody, and the pungent fragrance of the guava trees began to arouse my dazed and sleepy mind.

Did I have a horrible nightmare? Or is my husband really dead? What day is it? What are we doing today? Why is Nathaniel sleeping on the floor in our bedroom? Maybe if I close my eyes sleep will remove the gut–wrenching pain I feel.

Gradually I began to remember the events that had unfolded the previous afternoon. I had never longed for a nightmare before, but now I found myself desperately wishing that these traumatic events had been the narrative of a gruesome dream.

I curled into the fetal position. I wrapped myself in the beige comforter that Gary and I had bought with a 30%–off coupon at Kohl's in Colorado. I did not want to face this day when my husband's body would be placed in a Mexican furnace and burned to ash.

Carlos and Susana arrived sooner than we expected to drive us down the mountain to the crematorium. Carlos, being a businessman from Mexico City, was the only person we had met of Latin decent who was consistently early.

"*Hola, Rachel, ¿cómo estás?*" Carlos said as he kissed me tenderly on the cheek. "Did you sleep?"

"A little," I mumbled.

"How are your children?"

"Okay, I guess, we just want to get this day over."

Nathaniel, Bethany, and I crawled into the gray minivan with Carlos and Susana and headed toward Iguala. All the events surrounding Gary's death in a foreign country seemed raw and crude to my stateside sensitivities. Tragedy had catapulted Nathaniel, Bethany, and me into ongoing cultural challenges that we were not prepared to deal with.

We arrived at the crematorium, and my kids sat next to me on a stiff couch.

There were several Latino men around who appeared to work there. Eventually the undertaker walked to where we were seated, and with a stone–cold face said, "Your husband's ashes are too hot. The ashes need to cool before we can put them in a box. You must wait."

I sensed an evil presence that utterly unnerved me. These men seemed ghoulish and lacking in human compassion and tenderness.

Sometime later when the ashes cooled to an appropriate temperature, the undertaker tried to fit them into one of his standard containers but soon realized that a six–foot American male had a larger volume of ashes than a Latino man.

When he approached us again, chills ran up my spine. With a blank expression he explained, "There are too many ashes for our regular box. He was a tall man. You must pick out a larger box."

I walked over to a display case full of ornate, garish boxes. None of them remotely resembled something that Gary would have liked. My mind was a blur. Only twenty-four hours earlier he and I had sat listening to the song of the motmot birds, enjoying a quiet moment together. How could I possibly pick out a box to contain his bones and ashes? The thought was too bizarre for me to process. I could not emotionally grasp the decisions that my mind was being forced to make.

I chose a wooden box with the least embellishments—and I loathed it with a passion.

On the mountainous drive back to Taxco, important documents, along with the box of ashes, jostled on my lap in confused chaos. I attempted to balance everything but could not manage alone. Consumed with the terror of the past twenty-four hours, I feared that the paper stamped *muerte accidental* would be blown out of the window and Napoleonic law would render me guilty for the death of my husband.

Because of my irrational fear, I handed the box of ashes to Bethany in order to organize the official documents safely into a binder. Dressed in pigtails and capris, Gary's little girl steadied her daddy's warm ashes on her lap and kept them from lurching out of the box.

Regrettably, in my confused state of shock, I didn't realize the emotional burden I had placed on my young daughter who had just celebrated her fourteenth birthday.

Pulling into the cobblestone driveway, Carlos said, "Rachel, what do you need? We can stay with you."

"Thank you, we will be fine." At the time, I didn't realize the degree of untruthfulness this statement contained.

We exchanged the traditional kiss and thanked our friends as we stumbled past the entrance where Gary had died and into our beloved home that had been irrevocably altered.

I have no conscious memory of the rest of that day. It's as if my brain simply decided to stop recording the horrific details that had become my reality.

The following morning, I woke up and sipped a large cup of coffee but felt nauseated at the thought of food. Snuggled in Gary's sweatshirt, I sat down at our computer prepared to compose a ministry newsletter communicating the disaster that had befallen us.

When I began to describe the horrible events of his death, I started shaking uncontrollably. The horrendous shock and trauma of the past two days became too much for me.

"Nathaniel! Bethany!" I screamed, unable to stop shaking as I made my way carefully down the stone stairs to my bedroom. Instinctively I knew I should lie down. However, I never made it to the bed before falling face down on the red tile floor.

Nathaniel ran to the office phone and called Carlos. "Come to the house quickly. Something is wrong with Mum. I think she's dying."

I was lying on the floor going in and out of consciousness while our friends gathered around, and the scene felt horrifically familiar. A neighbor took my blood pressure and found it dangerously low. Somehow, probably because of Nathaniel's metabolic disorder, I had the presence of mind to think that this may be related to low blood sugar.

"Bethany, get me the chicken soup from the fridge!" I commanded in a short halting sentence.

Bethany ran to the kitchen in numb terror and tossed soup into a bowl.

My hands were shaking as I maneuvered a spoonful of broth into my mouth with most of it dribbling down over my chin.

"Mum, let me help you," Bethany said as she took the spoon from my trembling hands. And in a horrible reversal of roles, I lay helpless as my daughter fed me and dabbed my chin with a paper towel.

Eventually the soup had a stabilizing affect. Friends helped me crawl from the floor into my bed.

Once again, I remember nothing from the rest of that day.

Immediately after Gary's death a hush of reverence and honor seemed to fall on the barrio de Casallas. We saw the tamale man walking with his cart full of homemade delights but his familiar call of "Tamales!" no longer reverberated down the dirt road. The young man who rode his scooter carrying fresh tortillas from his grandma's stone oven no longer announced his arrival with a toot of a horn.

Nor did we hear the loud horn of Beto's *combi* when he drove into the neighborhood. Instead, he navigated the *combi* silently down the steep rutted roads, sharing the grief of our family and showing respect for Gary.

The ranchero music ceased. The street dogs stopped barking. It seemed even the roosters were silent in honor of *"misionero Gary."* The children did not play games or swing on the giant tree roots that clung to the hill behind their small concrete houses. Instead of the normal beautiful sounds of everyday Mexican life we only heard the explosion of complete and utter silence.

Our neighbors not only shared in our sorrow they also gave generously to our family. Tiny, wrinkled Indio women who only had a dry tortilla and a bit of salsa to eat each day came by and gave me warm kisses and stuck pesos in my hand. Others stood at our door with their large families hugging and kissing me and always giving me pesos.

No one knew our family's financial situation. They weren't aware that we didn't have the Mex$20,000 for the cremation, or that it was taking longer than expected for wired funds to arrive from churches in the States. The generous Mexican people didn't know whether we were affluent Americans or lacking in finances. Their love for us and their culturally ingrained value of generosity guided their actions.

When we went to church the same scenario repeated itself. Moms, dads, grandmas, grandpas, and children all hugged and kissed me and stuck pesos in my hand. They continually prayed blessings over our family and covered us in love.

The initial shock of Gary's death in a foreign country added to the trauma my children and I experienced, but the cultural aspect of love and generosity ministered profoundly to our wounded and aching hearts.

I was once again struck by the puzzling dichotomy throughout Mexico. This divergence was illuminated by the affection and altruism of our friends, neighbors, and churches, contrasted by the corrupt *federales* with their Uzis, the callous government officials, and the ghastly undertaker.

In the early days of bereavement my natural inclination during the agony of my soul was to isolate myself. Thankfully, however, friends continued to reach out to me through my self-inflicted isolation.

Every evening after Carlos left his office, he faithfully walked down our dirt road and brought respite to my pain–wracked heart. He quietly sat with me on the couch when I didn't feel like talking, and he listened to me when I needed to ramble. Though I often felt as though I couldn't bear seeing another human let alone being pleasant to one, those visits saved my life and brought a measure of sanity and normality where there had only been destruction and alienation.

Sergio, a man from church, stopped by our home with groceries every couple of days. His *bolsas* overflowed with simple staples such as toilet paper and dish soap, but he also brought plain Cheerios which became my go–to comfort food.

Others came with bags of sandwiches made with white Bimbo– brand bread and a little ham and mayonnaise. We appreciated these bland, familiar foods when we could not stomach tacos and enchiladas. I lost ten pounds in two weeks but thankfully was able to sustain some measure of health through these practical gifts of love.

One afternoon I was walking and stopped by the large aloe vera plants growing wildly in the tropical jungle behind our home. I felt

Gary's distinct presence, and I could see him in my mind though he was not present physically.

It's okay, Rachel, It's okay. It's okay, he said repeatedly with a rich and inexplicable smile.

Gary's response from heaven was characteristic of who he was as a man. I knew exactly what he meant. He wasn't referring to the glories of heaven being simply "okay." He was telling me that all the difficult times and the years of suffering that we had gone through were worth it in eternity. He didn't want me to grieve on his behalf. His face held a deep joy that I had never seen before, but he was completely himself as Gary J. Moore, my husband. This vision lasted all of thirty seconds and he was gone, but I knew he had come to me and I've never once doubted that it was him.

I have no theology that supports what I believe about this visitation. However, I do know it happened.

In quiet reverence I walked past the banana trees and back into my Mexican home pondering in my heart what had just transpired. It was years before I mentioned this to anyone. It was too sacred and beautiful to share.

A week after Gary's death, I invited the pastor from our church, Pastor Beto, over to our home. Pastor Beto knew very little English and because of grief I had lost my ability to speak in Spanish, so I had also invited Sergio, who kindly offered to translate for me.

As Pastor Beto and Sergio walked up to our front stairs, they trampled over the section of pavement where Gary had died. I felt distressed, as I often did, when that area was walked on as if it were ordinary concrete. I could not decide whether it was a sacred space or one of horror, but regardless it could not be void of meaning.

"Gracias, Pastor Beto, for coming to our home," I said.

"It is my pleasure," he responded warmly.

Kissing Sergio on the cheek I said, *"Hola, Sergio, ¿cómo estás?"*

"Ahhh, bien, bien. ¿Y tú?"

I walked them to the living room, and we sat down on the couches, one of which was the location where the EMTs had dropped Gary's body after he died. I tried to ignore the pain of these untouchable places being desecrated into ordinary usefulness. I knew in my head that it was just a couch and the concrete was just cement, but I could not convince my heart of those facts.

"I would like to have Gary's memorial service in our home." I addressed Pastor Beto. "I would be very honored if you conducted the service and shared God's love with our neighbors."

Sergio translated and Pastor Beto responded, "It would please me to do this for you. What day do you want it to be?"

"I was thinking next Friday, which will be a little more than two weeks since he died. I want to open the doors of our home and have everyone come in for the service and for sandwiches after."

Before Sergio translated, I said to him, "Is that appropriate?"

"*Sí, sí*, that is good," Sergio said.

"Oh, I'm glad, I wasn't sure how people do memorials in Mexico."

When Sergio shared my concern, Pastor Beto responded in Spanish, "Please don't worry, Rachel. What you have asked is very good. We will pray that many of your neighbors come to know Jesus."

"*Oh, muchas gracias, Pastor Beto, muchas gracias,*" I said, as my voice began to fill with emotion.

Everyone loved Gary, and our neighbors came in large numbers to our welcoming open door. Pastor Beto's son wrote a song of honor for Gary and sang it during the service. His dad gave a message of hope and salvation to our neighbors and friends. Every word that day was communicated in Spanish, and in my distraught frame of mind I understood very little. But our neighbor's hearts of love and friendship transcended language and culture.

Nathaniel and Bethany stood off at a distance. They felt invaded by the social aspect of eating and drinking while honoring their beloved father. We served simple sandwiches while everyone shared their love for us.

The tamale man expressed a desire to know Jesus. He talked and prayed with Pastor Beto and then deeply thanked me for Gary who brought God into his life. I was grateful for this precious man's newfound faith in God, but it brought little consolation to my sorrow–filled heart.

After the memorial service, life got back to normal in the little barrio de Casallas. We heard the little ones laughing and the teens dancing to the latest Latin pop song. Beto leaned on the *combi* horn whenever he drove into the neighborhood, and he blasted ranchero music from his concrete house down the hill. The roosters crowed, and the dogs barked. The joyous tamale man, with his newfound faith, called out as he pulled his cart of warm tamales up the road for his friends to savor and enjoy. And there was the occasional fiesta with raucous music playing throughout the night.

But for my children and me, Mexico would never be the same. The tropical flowers, the delicious food, and the people we loved had once been charming and lovely—now they were a backdrop to horrific loss and indescribable pain.

From Gary's death onward, it seemed like our life in Mexico was lived in a fog as if watching a fuzzy black–and–white movie from a hazy distance. Our minds would squint as if trying to see better, but very little was in focus.

Gary and Rachel's wedding, November 5, 1994.

The magic and beauty of the streets of Taxco.

The family's dearest friends, Carlos, Susana, and their beautiful daughter Camila.

Gary and Nathaniel playing chess while waiting for Rachel to cook their first spaghetti dinner in Mexico (the meal that led to Nathaniel's battle with typhoid fever!)

The rooftops of Taxco

Carlos, Susana, Camila, Gary, Rachel, Nathaniel, and Bethany
sharing Thanksgiving dinner together in Mexico.

Gary holding Carlos and Susana's baby, Sebastian.

*The gorgeous stone and brick living room after months of renovations
on the once–abandoned house.*

Gary and Nathaniel preparing for renovations on the old, abandoned Mexican house.

Sunny windows and Talavera tile graced the restored kitchen in the old,
abandoned house in Mexico.

Bethany and Camila

Susana, Carlos, Sebastian, and Gary

Five

THE SHOCK OF GRIEF

*"... his old life lay behind in the mists,
dark adventure lay in front."*

J.R.R. Tolkien, *The Lord of the Rings*

In Peter Jackson's brilliant movies based on J.R.R. Tolkien's *The Hobbit*, the Dwarves and Bilbo journey through Mirkwood Forest. As the dark magic in the forest takes its toll, our heroes find themselves lumbering forward in a gloomy haze, stumbling and lost. They forget all sense of instructions or logic. The forest takes over their ability to think clearly.

"Is there no end to this accursed forest?" Thorin says.

Similarly, I recall the weeks after Gary's death. My memories seem full of fog and mist as if we were trudging through Mirkwood Forest in Middle-earth. My kids and I were crying out for help, but our minds were in slow motion refusing to believe the tragedy that had unfolded before us.

Tolkien writes, "Bilbo found himself running round and round and calling, 'Dori, Thorin, Bomber' . . . while people he could not see, or feel were doing the same all around him. The cries of others got steadily farther and fainter, and though after a while it seemed to him they changed to yells and cries for help in the far distance, all noise at last died right away, and he was left alone in complete silence and darkness."

And that is the darkness in which we found ourselves.

There's really no way to describe what it's like to see the man that you've shared your spirit, soul, and body with writhe on the pavement, lose bladder control, and die suddenly while the motmot bird continues to sing and the air is laden by the sweet fragrance of guava.

I think of the utter darkness experienced by Helen Keller—not only visual but conceptual as well. Helen had no ability to define the blackness of her world. In fact, until the day Anne Sullivan held Helen's hand in the flow of a water pump and spelled the word "water" into her hand, Helen had no context for words or the meaning behind them.

When our family entered the silent darkness. No one traced the word "DEATH" in our hand in order to explain the sensations that we felt. The horror was too great and the shock too sudden to be able to identify any feelings in normal terms.

When someone dies, we typically do not disbelieve the reality of their death. I'm not saying families go on with life as if their loved one has not died. What I am saying is that there is a feeling of being detached from the profound implications of death.

When I looked at my husband's lifeless body and asked Carlos, "Is he gone?" I didn't say it with an outburst of emotion. And when Carlos wept and said, "Yes, Rachel, he is," I stood motionless and numb.

How the media portrays death is often a condensed version of a normal response to catastrophic loss. Movies often show an explosion of emotion at the scene of death rather than weeks or months later. Because our culture is strongly influenced by Hollywood we are bewildered when life does not reflect what we have seen on a screen.

The truth is that my initial response to Gary's death was a murky numbness.

In order for our emotions to be engaged we must have cognitive understanding of what has happened. When Gary died, I did not break down in an outburst of weeping. I was also not cognizant of my kids immediately after their daddy's death.

Many events of those early weeks when I could not function normally would come back to haunt me with shame and remorse.

I even found myself doing and saying strange and inappropriate things. I remember one day, leaning against the Telavera tile counter, saying to my grieving children, "Just think, we'll be able to go camping and Dad won't be there to complain about the lacking accommodations."

Ironically, as I write this, in the seven years since Gary has been gone, we have never once gone camping as a family of three. The pain of the fourth but empty sleeping bag is too deep and remains too raw.

The very disturbing aspect is at the time I believed I was responding logically. I wasn't trying to put on a happy face or look for the silver lining. I truly believed the ridiculous, unbalanced words that were coming out of my mouth.

The memory of those discussions with Nathaniel and Bethany are outlandish to me given the depth of love that we shared as a family. Months later when I came to my senses and realized what I had said, I felt an incredible amount of disgrace and self-contempt.

In time, I learned about the effects of grief, which helped me better understand that I was not capable of thinking rationally or functioning normally immediately after Gary's death.

In the previous chapter, I wrote about collapsing on the red tile floor of Gary's and my bedroom. The trauma was so great that my physical body felt completely overwhelmed. And while I recovered from that incident relatively unscathed, my emotions continued to be stuck in a murky never-land.

I cried many tears, but they were distant and full of confusion as if I were stumbling through Mirkwood Forest with Bilbo and the Dwarves.

I was disassociated from the horrific reality that had befallen our family. I functioned as needed and went through the motions of accomplishing tasks that I was required to do but I felt as if my body were not connected to my brain. I saw my life as though I were observing it from another dimension.

Hmm, that's odd. My husband's body was just cremated. I need to throw away his toothbrush and wash his laundry, I thought in a methodical fashion.

I observed myself abstractly and pondered, *Why is that crazy lady getting rid of Gary's clothes?* Or *Why do I have to make all these decisions? Gary is much better at dealing with factual details.* All the while, the logical part of my brain took care of specific tasks, talked to my children about grief, and comforted our Mexican friends.

In those first few weeks I joined an online dating site for bewildering reasons. On one hand, I was trying to fix the gaping hole in my heart and thought a new relationship would take the intensity of pain away. On the other hand, I felt irrational excitement about my new life and desired to dive into dating after eighteen years of marriage. *How many women who are devoted to their family and marriages have the adventurous thrill to begin again and to find love a second time around?* I pondered, as I posted photos on eHarmony of Gary and me arm-in-arm together!

In the nonsensical fogginess of my mind I was not functioning with reason. It was a bizarre action to join a dating site one week after my beloved husband's death, and to post photos of the two of us together was equally ludicrous. I snuggled in Gary's office looking through single men's profiles as if shopping for a new winter coat or comparing organic brands of breakfast cereal. The few who contacted me were fraudulent because emotionally healthy men were undoubtedly repulsed by the absurdity of my profile. I was deadened in my pain and shoved into an alternate reality with an inability to make rational decisions.

One month to the day after Gary's death my children and I enjoyed a wonderful respite in Zihuantanejo, a small Mexican fishing village. It was a beautiful remote location where we swam in the ocean, collected shells, and sunbathed on the soft tropical sand. I sauntered through the *mercado* in Zihuantanejo and delighted in my interaction with the local people. With a full heart I watched my children, who had been landlocked up until that moment, laughing and jumping in the ocean waves.

Months later, those joyful moments seemed almost sacrilegious. Had we forgotten that our husband and daddy had died? Where were our hearts? Where were our emotions? We were functioning as if Dad had gone to Mexico City for a ministry trip rather than being burned to ashes and bits of charred bone.

Emotional shock is the body's defense system. Its primary responsibility is to protect our mind from the annihilation of our lives that has just taken place. If we faced it all at once we would surely not survive the pain.

In the first six months I cried many tears, but I was living within the anesthetizing effects of emotional shock. This is the stage of grief where most of the misconceptions about bereavement are born. We who have lost a loved one are able to lift our hands in true worship. We laugh joyfully at a movie. We can counsel and comfort our friends. And many times, we are even able to experience frivolous and giddy thoughts about our future.

When others observe this season of shock, they think that we are doing wonderfully well. Our friends and family believe that we will continue our speedy path through grief and our life will soon be back to normal.

I often hear people say of those who have experienced loss, "Oh, they are doing remarkably well. They have gotten through their sorrow and are moving on with their life. I'm so proud of them for breezing through grief like this."

When someone dies outside of our immediate family or circle of close friends, we attend the funeral, cry our tears, and, within a few weeks, life for us is back to normal. We may feel sadness for an extended period when we are reminded of the person who has died, but our lives are not deeply impacted by the casualty. This is the frame of reference the general population has of bereavement. Therefore, we assume it is the same for those who walk through tragic personal loss.

The stories of people who appear to be sailing through the untimely death of a loved one are stories of victory told too soon. They are testimonies shared before the full realities of grief have even been experienced.

For those of us who have experienced great loss, the full weight of our grief will slam us into a wall, and our emotions will catch up with reality. By that time, the casseroles have been eaten, sympathy cards have been tossed aside, and our friends' hugs and prayers are a thing of the past.

The people around us are accustomed to our upbeat attitude. They aren't aware of the enormous surge of grief that hits months after we experience deep loss.

The most beneficial thing that we can do for our grieving friends and loved ones is to walk closely with them when the finality of death drops anchor and grief arrives for a lengthy season.

It is also imperative to be a voice of wisdom and protection over our loved ones when they are not able to think clearly. Disastrous situations with dire consequences can be averted if family members assume the initiative to be a protective voice of wisdom in the bereaved person's life.

I was a forty-six-year-old independent woman when my husband died. I did not easily submit to directives from my teenaged children or from friends in Colorado, so when people tried to help me, I often responded, "No, I'm fine."

But I wasn't.

I made costly blunders while attempting to figure out the future for myself and my children. One moment I bought moving boxes and airline tickets back to Colorado and the next day I ordered furniture from a local craftsman with stubborn determination to carry on the missionary work that Gary and I had begun together. I wasted thousands of dollars that I later would desperately need, simply because the trauma of Gary's death had impaired my decision–making ability.

In Proverbs 31 we read, "A wife of noble character who can find? She is far more precious than rubies. The heart of her husband trusts in her, and he lacks nothing of value. She brings him good, and not harm, all the days of her life" (BSB).

Gary had trusted me completely in our marriage and never doubted my ability to make prayer–filled decisions. He honored me for my wisdom and often spoke words of praise for how I managed our home and children.

When my husband died, our supporting churches in the States, as well as our friends and family, treated me with the respect and independence that I had earned throughout the years. What they didn't realize is that death levels the playing field and cripples a person previously filled with wisdom.

Books and seminars on grief encourage a person who has experienced loss not to make major life decisions for a full year after the death of a loved one. While I agree with this in principle, for most of us the very fact of bereavement creates the need to make rational judgments regarding our future.

When death itself requires level–headed thinking from a grieving person it is necessary for trusted friends and family to come alongside with wisdom, guidance, and prayer.

I find in Tolkien's books (and Peter Jackson's movies) so many powerful illustrations that seem to reflect my life. In *Return of the King* there is an unexpected villain. Denethor, the steward of Gondor, responds in deranged folly when told of his son Boromir's death. At one point, Gandalf comes along and whops Denethor with his wizard's staff trying to knock some sense into his irrational thinking.

This is a perfect portrayal of what many of us need during emotional shock. My children and I could never disagree with the fact that Gary had died in agony in front of our eyes. We could not, with any level of sanity, reject that fact.

Nevertheless, unbalanced thinking dominated our distorted reality. We urgently needed a wise and ornery friend like Gandalf to come along and knock some sense into our crazy thoughts and behavior.

The life experiences that push grieving people out of shock vary with each person and family situation. I felt the full weight of the reality of Gary's death when we made the move back to Colorado and our flight from Mexico City landed at the Denver airport and I saw the familiar Rocky Mountains.

January 19, 2013, six months to the day after Gary's death, the missions director from our church met Nathaniel, Bethany, and me at the Denver airport and drove us to our hometown of Loveland. The plan was for her to drop us off at the guest house of family we did not know well. We would be staying with them for several months until we could get settled.

Driving to Loveland from the airport, the conversation felt distant and cold to me as we related to her the facts of a missed flight in LA.

My children and I had departed the warmth of Mexico and the home where we had been a family, and suddenly we were catapulted into a Colorado winter among strangers. This was not the Colorado of our memory. What my children and I did not realize is that the idea of "home" meant "family"—and that our family had been burned up in a Mexican crematorium by a ghoulish undertaker.

Huddled in the back of the vehicle, we tried to remember the names and ages of the family who would be hosting us as the van sped north toward the ominous location.

"Is Sarah the youngest?" Bethany whispered. "What are the parents' names again?"

"I can't remember. Is Samuel the only boy, or is there another son?" I asked my children. They shrugged their shoulders.

The family had sent us a photo, and in the snapshot, the mother and daughters had been wearing skirts. *I hope our jeans will be appropriate,* I thought.

On and on we whispered to each other feeling the relief of finally being home comingled with the dread of living with strangers.

When we got off the highway and drove past the familiar outlet mall, a deluge of memories flooded my mind. Everything that my senses took in represented a family event that had occurred in our hometown of Loveland, Colorado. We had returned to all that was familiar but suddenly realized that there would not be a home without Gary.

As we drove through neighborhoods toward our destination, I thought back to a conversation the kids and I'd had a few weeks ago, when we were still in Mexico.

During that conversation, Nathaniel, Bethany, and I were talking about the happiness we would experience in returning to Colorado. The truth is, horrific loss had been our constant friend after Gary's death, and we had come to associate that pain with Mexico. *Coming home to Colorado will be our saving grace,* we had reasoned.

As we had talked together that afternoon in tropical Taxco, we had been surrounded by the mounds of Legos in Nathaniel and Bethany's collection.

Locating the Lego piece he'd been searching for, Nathaniel announced, "I can't wait to go adventuring at the sculpture park. Mum, we never told you, but we used to walk on top of the railing over the river."

I'd shaken my head. "I can't believe you guys did that. I don't think the statute of limitations has passed on that one!"

"Can we have a swimming pool in our new house?" Bethany had asked.

"Oh, I want a root beer float," Nathaniel said as he imagined his tummy grumbling.

Bethany scanned the massive amounts of Legos and found the mini-fig for her Lego family. "I would die for root beer. Oh, and ham. Mum, the first meal I want is real ham."

"Okay, okay," I'd laughed, while sitting down among the Legos. "Ham and root beer floats it is."

"That sounds gross," Nathaniel said.

Bethany had defended her culinary choice. "No, it doesn't. It's yummy. Christmas ham with root beer."

"Yeah, and that sounds gross," Nathaniel retorted. "Besides, its January."

"So? We can still have ham. Oh, and Mum's white sauce and potatoes."

Happy to see my children so full of hope I'd said, "Sounds good to me."

I picked up the small Lego house that I had created as a *casita* for Gary and me in the Lego town that had been built, broken apart, moved, and faithfully rebuilt many times throughout the years.

"Remember the Fourth of July you guys square-danced with Dad. . .?" My voice had trailed off as I thought about what it might be like to celebrate the Fourth of July in Loveland without him.

We had continued to discuss the wonderful memories, warmth, and love that our family had shared together.

Because of emotional shock none of us had made the logical connection that the empty ache in our hearts in Mexico would be exacerbated as we flew home to Colorado.

It simply hadn't dawned on us that all our memories included Gary and that his absence would annihilate the ability to recreate what had been.

We had carried on those conversations as if we could go back to life as usual in Loveland without a rational thought that Dad was no longer with us.

Now that our plane had landed in Colorado and we were in a van driving to an unfamiliar guest house in our hometown, the blunt reality was starting to sink in.

The missions director pulled her van into the long driveway, and our host family came out to greet us. I managed to remember all five of the children and their names as we shyly said hello and politely chatted before dragging our luggage inside the guest house.

The home was warm, cozy, and inviting. But as we settled in, we began to face the reality that Colorado would not signify the end of our numbing relationship with grief, but the beginning of an even darker season of unfathomable loss.

The reality consumed my thoughts that my husband was not coming home. My kids would never again run to the garage door anticipating his return from work. And at no time would he go to the store for bagels and come home with flowers for me. Gary would never again read Tolkien to our children nor plant a garden in the backyard. We would not stay up all night sharing our hearts, nor make love under the stars.

Nathaniel, Bethany, and I had come back to Colorado, but not to the home that we had once known. Colorado was cold, foreign, and desolate without Gary. We were no longer a family of four and, in many ways, it felt as if we were no longer a family at all. My children and I were suddenly aware of how unnatural it felt to be back home without Dad.

Our lives had been turned upside down and inside out.

Our competency in all areas of life had been severely impaired, including our ability to pray and feel the Lord's arms around us.

Many people casually said, "Just trust Jesus, he will comfort you." What they didn't realize is that when someone experiences catastrophic loss they are not functioning normally. As we stumbled through emotional shock, we could not easily feel God's presence or realize that he walked closely with us.

Nevertheless, looking back, I know without a doubt that he did.

And Scripture supports this.

After all, in Psalms we read, "He will cover you with his feathers, and under his wings you will find refuge; his faithfulness will be your shield and rampart" (Psalm 91:4).

When Jesus laments for Jerusalem, once again we see a word picture of being covered by the protective wings of God: "I wanted to gather your children together, as a hen gathers her chicks under her wings" (Matthew 23:37).

The psalmist says, "The LORD is gracious and compassionate, slow to anger and rich in love. The LORD is good to all; he has compassion on all he has made" (Psalm 145:8–9), and "The Lord is close to the brokenhearted and saves those who are crushed in spirit" (Psalm 34:18).

No matter what our bruised and battered emotions tell us at any given moment, God *is* our protector, provider, and comforter.

All through Scripture we are reminded of God's lovingkindness and his care for his children. He is a good Father and, in his graciousness, he carries us when the numbness of shock has immobilized our normal

Christian disciplines. He also is our mighty protector and keeps us from falling into enormously bad decisions.

Of course, we may have a difficult time wrapping our heads around this truth when we are deeply hurting, but that doesn't make it any less true.

Despite the murkiness and our stumbling through those initial months of shock, my children and I are absolutely convinced that God carried us and held our lives in a mighty and loving way.

We could not have survived the level of shock and the depth of our loss without our Heavenly Father holding us with gentle loving arms and covering us with his wings.

Six

THE DENIAL OF GRIEF

"Pays me what you owes me."

Gary J. Moore

G ary loved his children with a fatherly devotion. But it was not within his strong masculine nature to be delicate or nurturing.

When he would join Nathaniel and Bethany in a war game with Nerf guns he would never tread softly.

"Mum, come save us! Dad is pelting Nathaniel and me with his Nerf gun!" Bethany would yell as she ran giggling.

When Gary would play Monopoly with our kiddos, he did not let them win simply because they were his children. He would often say with joviality laced with seriousness, "Pays me what you owes me," as he gathered the spoils of a game well played.

In other words, being let off easy was not a perk of being a son or daughter of Gary J. Moore.

What I have discovered is that bereavement comes into our lives with a similar lack of nurturing. And in no uncertain terms, grief demands, "Pays me what you owes me!"

Everyone who goes through devastating loss grieves differently, but we all in fact must grieve.

In sports, there is a difference between defensive and offensive strategies. Emotional shock is the defensive reaction to loss. Denial, on the other hand, is an offensive reaction intended to help us power through the pain. But the truth is that these two game plans, while they might seem expedient at the time, make a destructive pair.

And the crazy thing is that—unlike sports teams that alternate between offensive and defensive strategies on the field—in grief, the coping mechanisms of emotional shock and denial can be operational at the exact same time.

Before ever returning to the States—while we were still experiencing emotional shock in our home in Mexico—I also experienced denial. Because of my passion for fitness, there were times I approached bereavement like an extreme sport. I thought, *If I can power through biking for ninety miles per week and lift weights that are beyond my normal capability, I will approach grief with the same tenacity and sprint through this quickly.*

I believed that grief could be cheated and therefore *should be* raced through by strength, speed, and persistence. *If I work hard enough and run fast enough the pain will go away*, I reasoned.

Therefore, I set out on a quest. I was on a mission to power through grief hastily and not allow this tragedy to affect my life for more than a few months. I devoured books on loss in order to meet my objectives. One book gave a checklist of things that must be accomplished during the first year after the death of a spouse.

Wonderful! Now I have a list, and the faster I work through the list the more quickly the pain will go away.

I read through each item in methodical order:

- Take off your wedding ring.
- Open the box of ashes.

- Go through personal items.
- Buy different furnishings and accessories.
- Open yourself up to a new relationship.

A few weeks after Gary died, I vowed to remove my wedding ring. I sat rigidly on the bed in our home in Mexico and contemplated what I was about to do.

At the same time, I couldn't focus. Everything felt monstrous and threatening in our bedroom. The box of ashes on the dresser seemed to fill the entire room with its menacing presence. The box demanded my attention. I could not take my eyes off it even as I tried to think about my wedding ring.

I said to myself in a forced mantra, *My husband is dead. I need to move on!*

My ring was a simple gold band Gary and I had bought at J.C. Penney in Pennsylvania. The ring had marks and scuffs on it from many years of gardening and cooking. I could hear in my mind how it clicked against our oak headboard when Gary kissed me. I visualized how my husband would lovingly touch my ring as he held my hand in prayer.

It's amazing how many memories from eighteen years of marriage can be evoked by one simple piece of gold.

I wrestled it over my knuckle and tossed it into a Mexican trinket container. I dodged the box of ashes and ran down the multi-hued stone stairway as sobs engulfed me.

Clearly sorrow occupied more of my heart than these outward actions would imply. Simply because I took my ring off after a few weeks did not mean that I had dealt with my loss.

This nagging thought in the back of my mind really sucked because I couldn't bear the piercing hidden thought that grief would demand more emotional currency than I wanted to pay. While other widows and widowers told me that it would take a lifetime to work through the various aspects of loss, I stuck my fingers in my ears and stubbornly said, *I'm not listening, I'm not listening!*

In fact, I wanted so desperately to advance and make progress that I continued following the list of things that the book stated I needed to do in order to get through the pain more quickly. I not only charged ahead with taking my ring off, I ran helter-skelter toward the next item on the list, which was to confront the box of ashes that I passionately loathed.

One week after removing my wedding ring I methodically walked into Gary's and my bedroom with the purpose of touching my husband's ashes.

The box was larger than I ever expected it to be.

The cremation process in developing nations is vastly different than it is in the States where there is a two-step process. Crematoriums in the US incinerate the body and then grind the pieces of bone into a coarse sand–like texture. In Mexico they do not grind the fragments, so little chunks and bits of bone make the ashes very coarse. As I've mentioned, I was repulsed by this box and hated it more than anything else associated with Gary's death.

I stared at it for some time. I didn't move. I didn't cry. I just glared at the box with burning eyes as if it embodied everything evil that had befallen our family. Finally, I cautiously removed the dark wooden lid and opened the twisty tie to the plastic bag inside.

I felt as if I were in a horror movie and some mutant demon would jump out at me.

I sifted my fingers through the ruins that once had been my husband's body. The ashes were coarse. They were a completely different texture than any ashes I had ever cleaned out of a wood–burning fireplace.

I came across a small fragment of bone and morbidly thought, *Is this the finger that turned the pages of his Bible—or maybe it was a cheekbone that held our children's soft babies' kisses?*

I could endure no more.

I quickly grabbed the twisty tie and wound it back up on the bag, replaced the lid, and sat the awful box back on my dresser. I silently scribbled a checkmark beside "ashes" on my list and ran into the shower so there would be no lingering residue touching me. I felt emotionally raped as if I had been violated by an evil predator. I needed to be clean and to be rid of the ravaging effects of death.

Much to my dismay, the act of touching my deceased husband's remains within the first month after he died did not remove one tiny speck of grief or eliminate grief's demand for a full and lengthy payment.

My stubborn tenacity to abolish the pain continued until six months later when we moved back to Colorado and the Rocky Mountains were once again the backdrop to our everyday routine.

For the first time since Gary had died, it began to sink in that this was going to be a long and painful process.

The memory of Gary was everywhere in Loveland because this is where we had shared our lives together. His presence was felt around every corner, in every store, and certainly at our house up the hill from Benson Sculpture Park on Banyan Avenue.

In despair, I began driving past the home that we had shared together—and had sold with many of our belongings before moving to Mexico—and stared from a distance into the windows. I felt like an orphan watching a dream that was now another family's life.

In addition, I walked and cried. Every morning during our six-month stay in the guest house of our new friends, I set out on the country road that meandered past it and walked for three miles.

Sometimes as I walked, I would double over and grasp my stomach as the intensity of gut-wrenching sorrow pierced me. The emotional agony was so deep that I literally felt pain in my body.

I cried out to God, weeping and begging my creator for a measure of relief. "Oh, God, help me. What am I to do? How am I to bear this awful torment? Oh, God, help me, please help me."

My emotions continued to unravel and after two months in Colorado I sat trembling in the guest house with PTSD unable to control the waves of panic rushing throughout my body.

Suddenly all my previous efforts came crashing down, and grief looked me sternly in the face and said: "Pays me what you owes me!"

My life came to a screeching halt, and I realized I could no longer cheat sorrow out of time and expression. Finally, I began the arduous process of paying grief the debt incurred when my husband's body lay crumpled and dead on the Mexican concrete.

Through this process I learned that the most important components of mourning effectively are time and expression.

We grieve poorly if year after year we are in the same exact place of sorrow but have not learned to give expression to our sadness through words or actions. We have given grief time, but we have not given it a voice.

We also grieve poorly if we rush into expressing our sorrow through actions such as removing rings or facing ashes. When we attempt to dash through our sorrow, we may have given grief a voice, but we have not given it time.

The two components of time and expression together bring the grieving ones to a place of eventual emotional and spiritual health.

Many widows and widowers assume that, because a tsunami of pain hit when their spouses died, if they quickly find another husband or wife, the waves will cease, and the waters of sorrow will rapidly recede.

This response has some basis in reality. When our vehicle is totaled in an accident, we remedy the upheaval in our lives by getting a new car. When a Colorado hailstorm destroys the roof of our home, we deal with the dripping water by calling a roofer. When our furnace goes out, we don't say, *I guess we'll freeze this winter* . . . No, we call the nearest HVAC company, and they come to our rescue with a new heating system.

In our desperation to get back to normal we seek to replace the thing, the loss of which has caused the disruption in our routine.

But what we don't realize is that, when we a loved one dies, replacing one person with another does no good. This is because what we have really lost is a *relationship*, and connections of the heart, when lost, can never be substituted or fixed; they must be grieved.

Part of the culture we enjoy as Americans is problem-solving. We are a great nation because we have overcome deep affliction and obstacles, discovering amazing solutions in the process. Entire careers are based on research and development. In business we are always streamlining and pursuing training that will teach us how to be more efficient.

We are not a fatalistic nation. We are a problem–solving nation. If we are sick, we take measures to get well. When we are in financial crisis, we look for a different vocation. If we are ignorant, we search for information. When we are overweight, we join a gym and so on.

When adversity strikes, citizens of Rome or Paris might cope by creating art by a river, but in America we problem-solve. We do not naturally turn to expressing our emotions when faced with an obstacle. In the States we power through and find a solution. Therefore, in the logical way of thinking as an American, it makes sense if we are suddenly widowed that we would strive to find a replacement.

In Ecclesiastes we read, "Two are better than one, because they have a good return for their labor: If either of them falls down, one can help the other up. But pity anyone who falls and has no one to help them up. Also, if two lie down together, they will keep warm. But how can one keep warm alone? Though one may be overpowered, two can defend themselves. A cord of three strands is not quickly broken" (Ecclesiastes 4:9–12).

The Bible is full of descriptions of the blessings of marriage. In Proverbs we are told that a man who finds a wife has favor from the Lord, and having her is like being showered with rubies. I've mentioned this verse before, but it is so rich with wisdom that it bears repeating here: "A wife of noble character who can find? She is worth far more than rubies" (Proverbs 31:10).

In Genesis God declared to Adam that it wasn't good for him to be alone. God initiated this statement. Adam wasn't sitting around complaining about his singleness. God brought up the subject, looking at Adam and announcing, "It's not good for you to be alone."

"The LORD God said, "It is not good for the man to be alone. I will make a helper suitable for him" (Genesis 2:18).

Marriage is a gift. It is a blessing from God. With all of heaven backing us why don't we put on our Nikes and sprint from the funeral luncheon to the wedding reception?

The reason is that there is a season for grief, and there is a time for remarriage. The Bible supports this idea of seasons. In fact, to paraphrase Ecclesiastes 3:1–8, there is a time for everything:

- A season for every activity under the heavens
- A time to be born and a time to die
- A time to plant and a time to uproot
- A time to kill and a time to heal
- A time to tear down and a time to build
- A time to weep and a time to laugh
- A time to mourn and a time to dance
- A time to scatter stones and a time to gather them
- A time to embrace and a time to refrain from embracing
- A time to search and a time to give up
- A time to keep and a time to throw away
- A time to tear and a time to mend
- A time to be silent and a time to speak
- A time to love and a time to hate
- A time for war and a time for peace

When we enter a new relationship too quickly, we are marrying for unhealthy reasons, and we cheat grief out of time and expression. A union after the loss of a spouse should never steal from the journey of grief that is set before us.

Some grieving men and women pour themselves into their careers, abuse mind–numbing substances, eat more than is healthy, or make continual expensive purchases trying to anesthetize their pain.

Many times, extroverts turn completely outward vomiting a never–ending stream of "Why me?" complaints onto anyone who dares to walk into their lives. Conversely, introverts turn inward putting up barricaded walls around their hearts and emotions, never allowing another human soul to touch them.

Most of us can recognize that abusing drugs or alcohol is not a wise life decision, but when the creditor of grief demands payment, what are we to do? How do we mourn effectively so that we are emotionally healthy for the next season of our lives?

I believe for most of us it is the price tag of time that we do not want to pay. Because truthfully while we are in debtors' prison to grief, we are also experiencing an enormous amount of pain. It is a concentration camp of torture, so naturally we want to break out and rush toward freedom.

We may resign ourselves to copious expressions of mourning—for a season. We may think to ourselves, *I don't mind torturous weeping for a year, but certainly I will not allow myself to be in pain for three years. I will consent to go to the grave site or scatter the ashes, but I will only do grief work for a set amount of time.*

And this is where we begin to cheat grief. There's no cap on the number of tears that are shed when we lose a spouse. There isn't a magic limit to the number of Kleenex piled on the floor when our baby dies. There isn't a predetermined timeline that we can follow when our young brother passes away from cancer.

The psalmist promises that God bottles up our tears: "You keep track of all my sorrows. You have collected all my tears in your bottle. You have recorded each one in your book" (Psalm 56:8 NLT).

This is an amazing passage of Scripture. It begs the question, however, whether God has a limit to the number of tears he will hold of ours until we must dry our eyes and suck it up. How many tears can be held in the bottle labeled "grief"?

The haunting questions become how do we know when we are cheating grief, and when are we overindulging grief with lavish gifts of time and resources? The problem is, we don't know. We have a creditor, but the bill is smudged, and we cannot read what is owed.

How do we measure anything when neither Metric nor English makes any sense?

Added to the exasperation of not being able to quantify the time that grief is demanding, we are also left with other unanswered questions. The method of expression within bereavement differs from person to person. Therefore, what does the day–to–day agenda of grief look like? How do we know if we are using the time well? What are the expressions of grief that can help us process effectively?

Being a missionary when Gary died, I learned to communicate the bullet points of our tragic story to the many people who needed to know. This habit of scratching the surface and ignoring what lay beneath proved to be a roadblock to complete healing.

For me, the depth of expression in my bereavement has been through the written word. As I have learned to write from the fullness of my emotions and relinquish my heart to the depths of sorrow, the composed word has given wings to grief, and much has flown away.

In a healthy approach to loss we must learn to express what is in our hearts and souls in some fashion. Grief cannot be approached cerebrally. Sorrow must be processed through our emotions and through the expression of our hearts.

Learning to feel and express our sorrow is always a personal journey. We may give voice to our grief through singing, journaling, or writing. We may find release through hiking, fishing, running, or climbing a mountain. The objective of these pursuits is to take the grief that has been shoved deep down into the recesses of our hearts and force it outside of ourselves.

Time heals all wounds is only true when the expression of grief is part of the passage of calendar pages falling to the ground. Otherwise weeks turn into months and months turn into years, and we are stuck in the agony of sorrow because we have never learned to get the pain that is on the inside of our soul outside of ourselves.

Once we concede to the time and expression necessary to feel the depths of our loss, we are then able to move forward in our bereavement in a healthy way.

We all must pay grief what we owe him. Sorrow cannot be cheated. There is a creditor who requires payment.

When we give grief time and expression, he will no longer have authority to come knocking on our door demanding, "Pays me what you owes me!"

Seven

THE TRAUMA OF GRIEF

"But this I call to mind, and therefore I have hope:
The steadfast love of the LORD never ceases;
his mercies never come to an end;
they are new every morning;
great is your faithfulness.
The LORD is my portion,' says my soul,
'therefore I will hope in him.'"

Lamentations 3:21–23 ESV

In previous chapters I described events of family joy and our delight in living in southern Mexico. Taxco was more charming and beautiful than I have detailed. Yet even before Gary's death we faced many unsettling circumstances. Some of these were stressful or frightening. Others were downright traumatic. We were in a constant state of hypervigilance, which contributed to anxiety and eventually to PTSD.

One such event during our first year in Mexico shook our lives to the very core.

It was December 11, 2011. Gary and the kids were visiting Carlos and Susana upstairs in their apartment for food and Xbox games. Because of a stomach virus, I had decided to rest on the couch downstairs while enjoying the sounds of their laughter echoing throughout our living room. Whatever game they had chosen seemed to be inspiring a lot of jumping and dancing, and at times it sounded like the armies of Cortez had been revived from their graves and were galloping to war above me.

Being in a quiet and reflective mood, I gathered a blanket and snuggled on the couch by our first Mexican Christmas tree. Full of thought, I looked at the stars through our open balcony doors and pondered what Christmas day would feel like in a tropical climate.

I felt what this evening needed was Christmas music, so I dug through our box of CDs and decided upon a traditional favorite by the Harry Simeone Chorale. Soon I was relaxing to the melody of *Silent Night*.

This night, however, would prove to be far from silent.

Suddenly I heard a loud explosive noise. I screamed, thinking that possibly Susana in her exuberance had jumped too hard and would soon be falling through the ceiling.

But the loud boom was not Susana in a freefall into our living room but the very earth itself shaking wildly below me.

The apartment building convulsed violently.

I heard our neighbors yelling in terror from every corner of the barrio and because of the explosive shaking I stumbled and fell to the floor.

I staggered to the door and opened it as if I were inebriated. I gripped the railing and saw Susana falling down the stairs in a dead faint while Gary and Carlos dashed ahead to catch her. Mass chaos ensued as our barrio gathered in the road to avoid falling debris and aftershocks.

Later we would discover that the epicenter had been in our state of Guerrero, and it was a 6.8 magnitude earthquake!

Our apartment building, constructed of concrete, did not sustain significant damage, but we all experienced ongoing anxiety from that terrifying event.

Another stressful experience was the continual challenge of fighting off dangerous villains who invaded our home. These were not human criminals but one of the deadliest species of scorpions. There was no area of our home sacred and protected from these awful creatures. We could not rest or relax a hand without being on alert. They were always waiting with their stingers ready to shoot deadly venom into an unsuspecting child or adult.

Added to these natural adversities was the very evil and active presence of the drug cartels. We knew of missionary families whose children had been abducted by cartels hoping to receive a bundle of American dollars.

While our beloved Mexican neighbors were kind and generous, the cartels were malicious and consumed with greed. It was not uncommon during a trip to Taxco for groceries for Gary and the kids to witness a cartel shoot-out.

In other words, life in Guerrero, while rich and beautiful, had not been without unprecedented challenges. Gary's death came after a long series of stressful events—and when it did, I felt like my breaking point had been breached.

I simply was not equipped to handle *one* more thing—especially not the greatest loss of my life.

Compounding the trauma, when Gary died, the faults within the tectonic plates below Mexico did not disappear, the scorpions did not pack their bags and leave, and the drug cartels did not stop their gang wars. We had no respite from the above-mentioned threats, despite being a bereaved family. For six months after Gary died, my children and I continue to live in the big old Mexican house that backed up to desolate tropical overgrowth. We were alone without any protection.

I functioned as normally as possible, but the cumulative effect of Gary's death—along with the ongoing dangers of life in southern Mexico—created wounds in me that had yet to be revealed.

It wasn't until my kids and I had been living in the guest house in Colorado for two months that I began to experience the full weight of the trauma we had suffered.

Sitting in the black recliner in the living room, my heart began racing. I felt sharp pains in my chest, and my whole body started quaking uncontrollably. My children stood close and watched in bewilderment. I felt terrified and had no idea what was happening to me.

This intense crisis response went on for two days. When these physical symptoms occurred, I believed that I was dying. This of course added to the anxiety and the abnormal way in which my body was functioning.

A friend drove me to the local urgent care center.

After a thorough exam the physician on duty explained to me that my heart was in perfect health. I was, however, suffering from severe anxiety and PTSD. The doctor, who was kind and compassionate, spent time describing how the body responds to trauma and what I could do to heal from the tragedy that had consumed my life.

Trauma has a wide range of sources and is certainly not limited to catastrophic loss and death. The dictionary defines trauma as "a deeply distressing or disturbing experience."

Often when we encounter this type of ordeal, we realize something awful has happened, but we don't have the language or experience to identify it. We are bewildered and shove the response deeply inward.

This is why emotional wounds can be cumulative. When we go through a traumatic event, we are not only dealing with the trauma of *that* experience—we are also dealing with the memories of traumatic situations in our past.

Past trauma creates within our minds a prolonged crisis reaction which can be triggered repeatedly from commonplace occurrences.

Triggers can include random things like hearing a loud noise, as well as stimuli such as too much caffeine.

Sometimes the most familiar everyday things propel us into panic. For example, in Colorado, I did not foresee the terror I would feel when going through a car wash, or how I would respond to the normal guttural sounds of a man lifting weights at the gym.

Plus, these triggers were so random and unpredictable that the fearful anticipation of my next panic attack filled me with even *more* anxiety. I felt betrayed by my own body and was tormented with the fear that I would become completely unraveled in a public situation. The thought of spontaneously reacting to some outside stimuli terrified me.

I became an expert at hiding not only my symptoms but also the emotional pain associated with PTSD.

If grief is the expected, predicable side of loss, trauma is the ugly unpredictable hidden side. I wept with grief on many occasions in public, but I did everything in my power to conceal a panic attack.

It would be years before I could function normally.

There is a distinct pathway for moving onward in grief, but trauma is more ambiguous.

For me, the first movement in my spirit toward restoration and healing was due entirely to God's power and presence. During the years when I was most wounded, healing came by resting in him and trusting his cathartic work in my life.

Sure, I faithfully went to church and maintained a semblance of a normal devotional life, but I believe healing was the direct result of the loving hand of God and was not brought about by my ability (or inability!) to adhere to Christian disciplines.

Traumatic events impact the physical pathways in our brain. As a result, another layer of my healing came through healthy eating, natural supplements, and exercise, which I incorporated into my everyday life.

A third layer of healing in my life came simply with time. Once when I was frustrated with a lengthy case of viral bronchitis, a physician friend said to me, "Rachel, sometimes the body just needs time to heal." And I believe that to be true of PTSD and anxiety. When the body and emotions are recovering from crisis, they need plenty of time and rest.

Finally, my journey toward restoration required the guidance of professional trauma counseling.

It's important to note that clinical anxiety and PTSD are not spiritual defects. The brain is a physical part of our body, and trauma affects the brain and changes the pathways. We cannot, by an act of will or prayer, change the concrete brokenness that living in a state of crisis creates. Emotional trauma does not require less attention than a physical malady—in fact, it may require more!

The good news is that our brains are amazingly malleable. Positive, hope–filled pathways in our minds can be reinforced and strengthened over time, while the grief–stricken pathways of despair can be healed.

This concept offers amazing hope for people who have experienced severe trauma. Through counseling we can learn the process that will rewire our brain out of the fight–or–flight response that tragedy has created.

It has been my experience that death is a tsunami, and trauma is the wreckage scattered on the shore when the waters recede. PTSD and anxiety were present from the moment we watched Gary convulse and die, but the emotions of loss were too powerful for us to see the enormous amount of debris left on the shore.

In her *Hakai Magazine* article, "A Tsunami of Trash," Ilima Loomis writes:

An estimated five million tons of debris was swept out to sea during Japan's 2011 Tōhoku earthquake and tsunami—five million tons of houses, cars, boats, fishing gear, shipping containers, and other materials. It was a catastrophic loss of property to add to the 18,500 dead. But where did all of this debris go? Beachcombers along the west coast of Canada and the United States reported finding fishing equipment, crates, and even whole boats in the years after the tragedy, but no one knew exactly how much had washed ashore.

This comparison accurately depicts what we experience emotionally in grief and trauma. We believe the initial storm is the most destructive aspect, but as life moves onward and the waters diminish, we are left to clean up the wreckage. And for some the process will take years.

I've experienced tremendous restoration in my life. In fact, the paragraphs above I shared with you four of the powerful influences—God's presence, taking care of my health and body, time, and professional trauma counseling—in my own healing. And great healing is more than possible—it is well within our grasp with the right resources and guidance.

But the reality is that remnants of PTSD and anxiety may follow us throughout our lives. Just like we move forward in grief we also move forward in trauma.

In Peter Jackson's screen rendition of *The Lord of The Rings* Frodo says to Sam, "How do you pick up the threads of an old life? How do you go on when in your heart you begin to understand. . . there is no going back? There are some things that time cannot mend. Some hurts go too deep that have taken hold."

It is important to accept the reality of catastrophic loss and what moving forward in our lives looks like. It's what we *do* with PTSD and anxiety as our companions that makes our life meaningful, not that they cease to exist.

Many times, we feel a desperate need to fight the lingering effects of grief and trauma in our lives. And yet, it is through these circumstances that we can truly embrace life with a deeper sense of meaning.

Men and women who have been through painful life events— the death of a loved one, abuse, war, devastating illness—are often celebrated for what they accomplished *despite* their pain, but I believe their accomplishments were very likely made possible *because* of their pain.

The verse that I chose for this chapter is about the hope we have in God: "But this I call to mind, and therefore I have hope: The steadfast love of the Lord never ceases; his mercies never come to an end; they are new every morning; great is your faithfulness. 'The Lord is my portion,' says my soul, 'therefore I will hope in him'" (Lamentations 3:21).

Our loving Heavenly Father's restorative power is ever working in our lives to bring us to a place of emotional health. No matter what we are facing, our hope is in him. We have a Heavenly Father who loves us beyond our wildest imaginations. If we could grasp even a glimpse of God's love for us our lives would be deeply impacted and forever changed.

Occasionally God moves in the miraculous, and where there once was complete devastation there is complete restoration. But often the Lord takes us on a lengthy journey of healing.

Does this mean that we are broken?

Well, yes, but we are sweetly broken before the Lord.

The Bible has beautiful things to say about brokenness. The psalmist says, "The sacrifices of God are a broken spirit; a broken and a contrite heart, O God, you will not despise" (Psalm 51:17 ESV).

"The Lord is near to the brokenhearted And saves those who are crushed in spirit" (Psalm 34:18 NASB).

The prophet Isaiah spoke of Jesus who would heal and care for us in our brokenness. "The Spirit of the LORD God is upon me. . . he has sent me to bind up the brokenhearted" (Isaiah 61:1 ESV).

We know that we are his children, and because of his love for us, we can lie back in his loving arms with belief and trust in the healing work that he is doing in our lives.

Eight

THE ANGER OF GRIEF

*"'Lord,' Martha said to Jesus, 'if you had been here,
my brother would not have died.'"*

John 11:21

The stages of grief are not linear steps but alternate widely in the random way they invade our lives. If truth be told, the various aspects of grief can ambush us at different times all in one day. When we experience loss and trauma, we are surprised to find our journey is not tidy and predictable.

Many of us who have a personal faith in God are afraid to face the anger associated with healthy grieving. We may believe in our hearts that what happened to our loved one is unjustifiably wrong but struggle with the dichotomy between anger and faith. What we need to realize is that anger is a normal part of bereavement and is not indicative of a character flaw, sin, or deficiency.

Surprisingly, I had to confront deep anger toward Gary for leaving me. This sounds ludicrous, but often there is a natural resentment toward the loved one who has died and the feelings of abandonment that go along with untimely death.

At different times I spoke aloud to Gary, not believing I was conversing with the dead, but letting out my negative emotions and outrage because of his death.

"How you could you leave? How could you abandon Nathaniel and Bethany? Didn't you love me enough to stay with me?" "How am I supposed to finish well with our children when I am totally alone? How could you desert Nathaniel, Bethany, and me and leave us behind in southern Mexico?" "Why didn't you tell me you were not feeling well? Why did you hide what was happening from me? Why didn't you tell me that you felt you were dying?"

Eventually, I would break down in deep sobs of sorrow and in my tears, I spoke words of respect and forgiveness toward Gary.

Many times people believe that the outburst of anger will be a onetime event. In my experience—and in the experience of others who have survived similar losses—anger comes in waves through the ongoing journey of grief.

The solution to dealing with anger during our bereavement is once again time and expression. If we stuff our negative feelings deep in our hearts, they will begin to poison our lives and, like rotting bones, will come back to haunt us.

Time alone does not heal, and expression alone does not heal, but time and expression together can be a cathartic *combi*nation.

What happens, though, when the person we are most angry with is ourselves? Will time and expression rid our soul of the toxicity of anger against our own frailties?

When Gary died of sudden cardiac arrest, I was appalled that I had not recognized the signs that something was wrong with my beloved husband prior to his death. It was agonizing for me to accept and forgive my medical ignorance. I had to conclude that I neither had the power nor the wisdom to add or take away from Gary's life.

A further facet of anger against ourselves is the feeling of shame and regret for how certain dynamics of our relationship had played out.

We can find ourselves plagued by remorseful thoughts.

Why didn't I tell her I loved her more often?

I should have showed more respect.

I should have expressed my admiration for him.

Why did I fight with my husband over silly things?

I should have played with my little boy rather than fold laundry.

Why didn't I dance with my little girl?

In the movie *Courageous*, the main character's nine–year–old daughter dies in a car accident. The grief–stricken father painfully remembers a conversation in which he refused his beautiful daughter's plea to dance together in a parking lot:

Dad: Emily, what are you doing?

Emily: Dance with me, Daddy.

Dad: This is a parking lot. This is not where people dance.

Emily: Just for this song? Please?

Dad: Emily, people can see us.

Emily: That's okay, they don't care, Daddy, please?

In a poignant scene after her death, Emily's father goes back to the parking lot where she had begged him to dance with her. He begins to move his feet to her favorite song as he pictures his daughter with him. This is a healing moment as he is able to begin the process of transforming that painful memory into something precious.

Processing aspects of our relationship with the person we've lost is a fundamental aspect of the journey of grief. The antipathy directed inward needs to be forgiven just as the animosity outward needs to be forgiven. Going through external actions, such as what the father did in the movie *Courageous*, can bring expression to our regret and healing to our hearts.

What happens, though, when we experience anger at God himself? What is our response when Jesus shows up to the location where our loved one's blood is flung on the pavement and we are crushed that he didn't bother or care enough to arrive sooner? What happens to our faith? To our relationship with God?

God, where were you when Gary was dying on the concrete? I prayed for you to rescue our family, but you didn't. . .

In my journey of grief and loss, the first time I experienced anger at God happened after we moved from Mexico back to Colorado. It had been six months since Gary had died, and the kids and I were staying in our friend's guest house in the town where Gary and I had raised our family and spent most of the years of our marriage. One evening I was driving home from the grocery store when my car naturally turned onto Banyan Avenue, toward the home where Gary and I had built our family together.

The February wind was cold and blustery as I pulled to the curb in front of the house. I saw the green mailbox Gary and I had bought at Home Depot on a Sunday afternoon, and the flower bed, now covered in snow, that we planted after lifting sod on Mother's Day.

My gaze swept over the barren grass and lingered on the little pine tree that we had decorated each Christmas, then on the empty spot where our swing used to sit.

Still sitting in my car, I looked through open curtains into rooms aglow with warm lighting and began to observe the family who had purchased our home. Downstairs, I could see a father and children in the living room.

Then, looking up, I saw the master bedroom window flicker with the glow of candles. Was the wife in Gary's and my shower, freshening up for a romantic evening with her husband? I knew every corner and inch of that room. Was their bed under the window like ours had been? Did she buy her bathroom towels at Kohl's with a 30%–off coupon as

I had done? What would she wear for a romantic evening with her husband? Did her husband delight in her as mine had delighted in me?

I saw children downstairs in our living room doing their homework. Maybe they had just finished building Legos with their dad before they had to get to their studies. I could see a couch in the same place where we had put ours. Did this family have movie nights with popcorn like we did? Did they put their Christmas tree in front of the window where ours had stood? Did the walls echo with love and laughter as they had done for so many years when our family lived at that address?

I could take the agony no longer and lurched the car into drive and sped away, back toward the guest house. Seeing a family joyfully living in our home had brought deeply buried anger to the surface.

As I drove, I cried out to God. "No! It's not fair! It wasn't supposed to be this way! No, God, no!"

I continued my lament while quaking sobs filling my body. "We were serving you on the mission field. How could you let my husband die?"

I banged angrily on the steering wheel with my fist until I feared that it would break in two. "Gary loved you with all of his heart! Why did you let him die? What are my kids and I to do? How can we possibly bear this horrible pain?"

I don't know how I made it safely back to the guest house as I was emotionally distraught and could barely see through my tear–filled eyes.

It wasn't until several years later that I could acknowledge how angry I had felt at God.

In the Bible when Martha is overcome with grief over the death of her brother Lazarus, her words to Jesus communicate feelings of betrayal and anger. "Lord," Martha said to Jesus, "if you had been here, my brother would not have died" (John 11:21).

How many of us have said similar words? "God, where were you? If you had been here my baby would not have died, the car accident would not have happened, or the cancer would have been healed."

After her brother's death, when Martha's thoughts turn toward Jesus, he almost seems like a self-absorbed upbeat friend who is more concerned about supplying the beverages at a wedding than the tragedy that has befallen her family. Martha had seen Jesus do incredible miracles of healing; she knew he could prevent death—*but that he had chosen not to.*

In our own lives we believe Jesus is powerful to heal and deliver but often he seemingly ignores our pain and shows up a little too late, just as he did with Mary and Martha. Because we imagine Jesus's actions as a lack of love as well as a horrific oversight his part, we feel God capriciously allows pain into our lives.

In our hearts we feel Martha's lament. How do we trust a God who has the capability to heal and protect from disaster but chooses to arrive late at the hospital bed? What do we do with this anger directed toward the creator of the universe and the beloved savior of our souls?

If we are honest with ourselves, we have to admit that sometimes anger sucker-punches us and bruises the very core of our spirits.

We feel bewilderment regarding the father-heart of God in light of the cruel loss that we have suffered. We are not able to comprehend his sovereignty over our lives, and confusion becomes an obstacle to our faith.

Is God surprised by our anger?

Absolutely not.

God already knows our thoughts, and his love, grace, and mercy covers us even in the darkest moments of our emotions.

David laments throughout the Psalms:

How long, O LORD? Will you forget me forever? How long will you hide your face from me? How long must

I take counsel in my soul and have sorrow in my heart all the day? How long shall my enemy be exalted over me? (Psalm 13:1–2 ESV)

My God, my God, why have you abandoned me? Why are you so far away when I groan for help? Every day I call to you, my God, but you do not answer. Every night I lift my voice, but I find no relief. (Psalm 22:1–2 NLT)

"O God my rock," I cry, "Why have you forgotten me? Why must I wander around in grief, oppressed by my enemies?" Their taunts break my bones. They scoff, "Where is this God of yours?" Why am I discouraged? Why is my heart so sad? (Psalm 42:9–11 NLT)

Lament opens the heart and voice to tell God what's really happening inside our souls. He bids us to be intimate with him and he desires to hear the expression of our soul. We are to go to him as Abba Father, as Daddy. And sometimes approaching him as our dad means yelling, stomping, and pitching a fit. We can get ugly with God; he can handle our painful emotions.

In part, our anger is caused by our human inability to comprehend the expanse of who God really is. We believe that he should act in ways that we can easily figure out and understand. We imagine the trinity to be only slightly smarter than ourselves and therefore we assume God is going to act with something akin to human logic—in other words, not too differently from how we would.

We diminish our creator so that we can understand him, but when adversity catapults us on a journey outside of our well–ordered logical plan, we wonder if he is good or if he even exists at all.

"A god small enough to be understood," the British philosopher Evelyn Underhill observed, "will never be big enough to be worshiped."

What we need to realize is that a god who can be understood is not god at all but a mere human who is as weak and fragile as we are.

When we reduce God to a being that we can comprehend, we have stripped him of everything we need him to be. If our God is small enough, we will climb up on his lap and snuggle in his arms. However, if he is not large enough to hold the universe in its place, we cannot count on him any more than we can count on a kindly grandpa who wishes he could make our lives better but is powerless to do so.

In comic book terms, we tend to think of God with the power and might of Superman but hindered by the common human attributes of Clark Kent. He may be very lovable and endearing, but he tends to mess up a lot when trying to heal our spouse from cancer, or prevent a loved one's suicide, or save our baby from drowning.

As J.D. Greear says in his book *Not God Enough*, "When life caves in on you. . . you need more than a sentimental Jesus sitting beside you stroking your hand, explaining that there's a silver lining or spewing nonsensical platitudes about things that don't kill you only make you stronger. You need a God of infinite glory who sits upon the throne of the universe, who has promised to marshal every molecule in the universe in pursuit of his plan and your good, who stands behind your salvation and will let nothing stand in his way."

In Isaiah we read, "'For my thoughts are not your thoughts, neither are your ways my ways,' declares the LORD. 'As the heavens are higher than the earth, so are my ways higher than your ways and my thoughts than your thoughts'" (Isaiah 55:8–9).

What we need to realize is that God's design is so far above our own that we cannot even begin to comprehend it. We believe in his might, but we also need to believe in his intellect and reasoning. If God can speak to dirt, breathe on it, and create a human out of absolutely nothing, surely his cognitive ability is far above my capacity to judge.

When we are face to face with horrific loss the only thing we can understand is that we cannot possibly fathom God's ways. And when we come to terms with this, we can begin to accept the fact that God is good all the time. When we accept that our good God can have ways and thoughts that we cannot grasp, our faith is restored and we can once again trust him.

And sometimes trusting him means going to a funeral.

Often, people try to resolve this dichotomy with platitudes and clichés. But these fall short when trying to explain the unexplainable.

Yes, one Mexican man gave his life to Jesus through Gary's memorial service, and his newfound faith is of great eternal value. But we were on the mission field giving our lives for the gospel. It would stand to reason that Gary would have led far more men, women, and families to the Lord through a long life lived in southern Mexico than he did by dying.

When a child dies, the family may be drawn more deeply into the Lord. When a spouse suffers with cancer we may learn to pray more often. If a young gal's mama dies, she may lean into Jesus more than she would have otherwise.

But are any of these areas of spiritual growth worth the profound price of death?

We may gain patience or a deeper prayer life when our loved one dies. But do we really believe that God goes around killing our husbands and children so that we have more patience while driving in traffic?

That is a ludicrous thought, and yet so many times this is the type of comfort our insipid, nonsensical thoughts can give to us.

Does this type of illogical thinking help to appease our anger? Absolutely not! Nothing works to make sense out of our anger better than a simple but powerful acknowledgment that God's ways are not our ways.

I am convinced that God's story as well as our own includes all of eternity, not just the short moment of our life here on earth. Our memoir does not end when we die. In many ways our life here on earth is only the first chapter. Therefore, everything that happens to me doesn't just involve my life in Colorado. It also affects the spirit realm and everything that is transpiring in eternity.

According to Paul, our suffering on earth is of eternal value. He wrote, "So we do not lose heart. Though our outer self is wasting away, our inner self is being renewed day by day. For this light momentary affliction is preparing for us an eternal weight of glory beyond all comparison, as we look not to the things that are seen but to the things that are unseen. For the things that are seen are transient, but the things that are unseen are eternal" (2 Corinthians 4:16–18 ESV).

What we conclude from this is that our horrific loss is important, it counts, and it accomplishes something grand and amazing in eternity. We don't understand what that is yet, because we cannot comprehend heavenly matters.

But one day it will make sense, and we will see the significance that our baby's death held. We will understand the noble cause that a brother dying of cancer accomplished. We will know and see the amazing ways that God's glory has been manifest through the death of my husband. We will see all these magnificent things, and we will finally understand and give praise to our Heavenly Father.

We will no longer say, as Martha did, "Lord, if you had been here my brother would not have died."

For we will understand the *eternal weight of glory* that was created because of the tragedy that we have walked through.

Gary will run up to my children and me with arms open wide and say, "It's okay, it's all okay, look what our savior has done!" and then we will see the eternal weight of glory manifested from his death.

We read in Corinthians, "For now we see only a reflection as in a mirror; then we shall see face to face. Now I know in part; then I shall know fully, even as I am fully known" (1 Corinthians 13:12).

Everything will make sense and we will see openly the hand of God in the suffering of our souls. We will fall before our savior and worship Jesus because we will see clearly and understand fully.

Nine

THE DEPRESSION OF GRIEF

"Hope deferred makes the heart sick,
but a longing fulfilled is a tree of life."

Proverbs 13:12

When a spouse dies, it's possible that the bereaved husband or wife has hidden thoughts of things they will look forward to after they stumble through the darkness of death.

This is especially true when there has been a lengthy illness.

The remaining spouse may decide to paint the house or buy fresh bedding. Anything new feels wonderful and works to remove the weight of death from the heart and home.

One widower secretly confided in me the lighthearted delight that he experienced while traveling to a peaceful oceanside resort with his children. He said to his son, "Is this what life can be like without cancer?"

He had been in the world of the dying for so long that it brought incredible freedom to feel the sunshine on his face, taste the salt of the sea on his beard, and to rediscover how wonderful our world really is.

And this doesn't apply only to those who have suffered with a loved one through a long illness. Even those of us who have experienced the sudden death of someone we love can find ourselves thinking about the future with a measure of anticipation.

I have met people who are bewildered by these emotions. In fact, sometimes my emotions bewildered me. How could I feel anticipation and happiness when my heart was so broken?

As I mentioned earlier, when a spouse dies, the emotional response of shock and denial can create within our murky emotions the feeling that we are still married. It feels as though our husband or wife is on a business trip or visiting a distant relative. We may expect them to text or to open the garage door and take out the trash before coming inside.

As you can imagine, when we feel that we are experiencing a temporary parting, it evokes a very different response than we would have if we fully grasped the permanence of our separation.

In the movie *Home Alone*, Kevin, the character played by young Macaulay Culkin, finds himself. . . well, home alone for several days. He spends the first day eating ice cream and watching junk TV. Knowing that eventually he will be reunited with his parents, he takes the opportunity to enjoy all the crazy antics that his parents would not have allowed had they been home.

We can enjoy the fun of this movie because we also know that Kevin's separation is temporary and that he will be reunited with his family in short order.

Obviously eight-year-old Kevin would have been doing, saying, and feeling vastly different things if he were home alone because he had been suddenly orphaned.

When a spouse dies, against all logic we may not be able to fully grasp the idea that the separation is permanent (at least this side of heaven!) If this is the case, we may find ourselves perplexed by the lightheartedness of some of our thoughts, words, and actions.

Because of this—like Kevin—we can enjoy a freezer full of ice cream and an open door to whatever adventurous antics we may desire just weeks after the death of our loved one.

This is why grieving people are warned not to make any big decisions following a major loss. Some people, ignoring this advice, embrace a rapid marriage to an alluring person or an impulsive move to a tropical location simply because the sun sets beautifully over the ocean every evening.

When the shock wears off, we may look at our decisions and think, *My God, what have I done?*

Reeling from the aftermath of our "inappropriate" emotions (and perhaps even from the results of a few hasty decisions) we may find ourselves in the grip of an unexpected foe—and its name is depression.

Before the shock wears off, we're able to promise ourselves and our children that tomorrow will be better. And we believe it to be true. But after the initial shock fades, depression can set in as we face the harsh reality that we have only begun to grieve and that life will not be returning to normal tomorrow—or many tomorrows, for that matter.

Unable to see the light at the end of the tunnel, we can lose all hope.

In Proverbs we read about the connection between a lack of hope for our destiny and the darkness of depression: "Hope deferred makes the heart sick, but a longing fulfilled is a tree of life" (Proverbs 13:12).

In this stage of grief, we are no longer able to continue our daily powerful pep talks of who we will become and what benefits life after grieving may bring.

Regardless of how optimistic a personality we might typically have, nothing can keep us from experiencing all the of stages of grief—*and depression is an unescapable stage of grief.*

We should not be perplexed when this happens.

Nevertheless, three years after Gary's death, depression completely blindsided me.

For three years, I had consistently believed that the next day, week, month (and certainly the next year!) would bring healing and that our pain would go away.

In the meantime, I exhausted myself trying to make up for my children's loss. Not only was I faced with learning a new profession in real estate but, as a widowed mom, I thought it was my job to take away my children's pain.

Most mornings, I would make elaborate breakfasts for my kiddos, even though three was such a lonely number around our table.

Despite my lack of Lego skills, I often joined Nathaniel and Bethany in their creative endeavors as Gary had once done.

I planned outings to movies, the ballet, and trips to a beautiful resort cabin in the mountains.

I bought a swimming pool for our back yard in hopes that it would bring joy to my children as it once had done when Gary had been with us.

Dinner became a special family event as I tackled one delicious in–depth recipe after another trying to add enthusiasm to our rather dismal family meals.

I stayed up late on many December nights painstakingly planning our special Christmas traditions, including holiday concerts, gifts, and a large and full feast, even if it was only for three.

And on the second anniversary of the terrible afternoon their daddy lay dying, I was certain my children could be cheered by a trip to the Denver Botanical Gardens.

For three years, I had been determined that my children and I would not only survive our tragic loss, but that the three of us would remain bonded by the traditions we had once shared with Gary.

I had been desperate to create a joy–filled and loving home for my kids, despite the ongoing ravaging effects of grief upon our lives.

I had dug my feet into the ground and resolved that grief *would not* steal my family!

Unfortunately, what I did not understand was that my family had already been stolen when Gary lay dying on the pavement while the motmot bird sang and the breeze rustled through the brightly colored bougainvillea.

It took three years, but I discovered, late in the game, that it is *impossible* and even sometimes *damaging* to force family traditions to go on as they once had after a loved one has died.

I finally understood that regardless of my valiant efforts, I had not succeeded in recreating one tiny aspect of our family's previous life or the happiness that we had once shared together. Every carefully planned family event was haunted by the desolation of death and ended up being ruined by the depth of our mutual pain.

I also understood, finally, that despite my optimistic nature, my world and the world of my children had been irrevocably destroyed.

It was at this moment when I fell deeply into depression.

I wanted to run from this new enemy.

What I needed to do instead was face it and wrestle with it.

In Tolkien's *The Fellowship of The Ring*, our heroes are being pursued by something that is straight out their darkest nightmares. Instead of running, the wizard Gandalf stands bravely before the evil balrog and confronts him face to face. While it appears that the balrog gets the upper hand, we see later that their interaction has made Gandalf much stronger and more compassionate.

Many people run from their depression because they are terrified by the thought of facing their anguish. Like the balrog, depression is an enemy so awful we are certain we will be consumed by it, when in reality our interaction with our pain will make us stronger and more compassionate in the end.

It takes courage, boldness, and heroism to face our grief head on. Working through depression rather than running from it is one of the most honorable and praiseworthy things that we will ever accomplish.

I think one of the reasons depression can be so difficult to admit and face is that we think it conflicts with faith.

When our lives are consumed with depression and grief, we may be tempted to berate ourselves with the thought, *But where is your faith? Where is your joy in the Lord?*

After all, in the familiar verse we read, "'For I know the plans I have for you,' declares the LORD, 'plans to prosper you and not to harm you, plans to give you hope and a future'" (Jeremiah 29:11).

I have discovered however, that we can agree with Jeremiah in our spirits that God has a plan and a hope for our future, but we process the carnage of our life with our minds and emotions.

In other words, faith is expressed through our spirit, while emotions are expressed through our soul. We must realize that the emotions of loss are as real and tangible as our faith.

When I think of how our spirits and emotions (and even our bodies) can operate independently from each other, three examples come to mind.

The first thing I think about are the months prior to Gary's "sudden" death.

I think of that entire season as "the months when Gary was dying." I think of it this way because I truly believe that unknown to us at the time, his heart had been failing for some time before he died.

During that time, exhaustion conquered his body. He also battled deep inner turmoil because he was not able to keep up with normal ministry tasks.

Yet while these things were going on in his body and emotions, Gary's spirit was overflowing with joy, and his preaching was anointed with the presence and peace of God.

I find another example of the dichotomy between spirit and emotions when I read the story of Mary, the mother of Jesus. I have no doubt that she experienced a separation between her own spirit and emotions.

After all, in Luke we read that Mary proclaimed that her spirit rejoiced in God her savior. But how did her emotions respond to being unwed and pregnant? Was she frightened? Was she afraid that her beloved Joseph would abandon her with a baby that was not his own? Did her pregnancy make her feel sadness, nausea, or exhaustion?

Scripture says that her spirit rejoiced but doesn't mention what a mess her hormone–driven emotions may have been in.

Finally, I find it astonishing that on the night before he was crucified, while Jesus's faith did one thing and stayed steadfast, his emotions took quite a different path.

On the evening prior to his crucifixion, Jesus knelt before the Father. Condemned to death, he pled to be released from what lay before him. After a night of anguish during which he sweat great drops of blood, he was led away by soldiers to be tortured.

Jesus knew the plan of redemption, and his faith was solid and unshakable as he walked in relationship with his Heavenly Father. His emotions, however, were impacted greatly by the human experience of dread and sorrow.

We can experience the same thing that Jesus did. Our spirit, which is the part of us that connects with God, may be overflowing with joy. At the same time our soul, which is the emotion–based part of us, can be sucker-punched with sorrow.

Is it possible that the scriptural command to "rejoice always" is directed at our spirits and not our minds or emotions?

As humans, we cannot fall under the misconception that only our spirits deserve a voice.

We must walk in unity with the trinity of our personhood. This is how depression and faith are able to coexist, even in the heart of a strong believer.

To make matters even more difficult, when we do share with others the agony of our soul, we may encounter responses that are not helpful—especially from believers who expect to hear only from our spirit.

These folks may celebrate our progress through grief when our spirit swells with the intensity of worship and our hands are raised in praise to the Lord.

At the same time, they may not understand when we are feeling the dark emotions of depression. They don't understand how we can experience faith and depression at the same time.

Here are some examples of the kinds of comments that can be made when someone doesn't understand how our spirits and emotions can operate independently of each other:

> "My friend's husband died two years ago; she seems to be so depressed lately. I don't feel she is trusting the Lord."

> "His wife died a year ago. I cannot believe how dark his emotions are. I think he is in bondage and needs to be delivered."

> "It's been a few years since the diagnosis, and I am concerned because she seems to be more depressed now than when the cancer first hit. I don't think she is walking in faith."

> "I'm glad she's pregnant again after her baby's death. This will help her to have the joy of the Lord and not cry so much."

These kinds of messages—even from well–meaning people who love us dearly—can make us doubt ourselves.

Do I need to have more faith?

What's wrong with me that I feel this way?

Is God disappointed with me?

But we must realize that the stages of grief—*including depression*—weave in and out of our journey of loss. We should not be surprised when this happens. We cannot cheat the season of depression any more than we should try to cheat acceptance and moving onward.

Giving our grief the time and expression that it requires is the pathway through depression.

Built into lament is the necessity of getting our pain outside of ourselves. We tend to think that talking about our pain with friends, pastors, or counselors is the only way to do this, but it's not.

So what does this look like?

Outward expression may also include grieving alone in the mountains or through poetry or song. Outward expression may include lifting weights or running a marathon. And sometimes a remote mountain lake is the most comforting repository for our deepest expressions of sorrow.

Ultimately, release from depression has its foundation in God as we ask him to show us his hope–filled promises for our future.

In Romans we read, "May the God of hope fill you with all joy and peace in believing, so that you will abound in hope by the power of the Holy Spirit" (Romans 15:13 NASB).

We have joy because God is a solid foundation, and his promise is for abundant life. But how do we grasp hold of his desire for our destiny despite catastrophic loss?

Throughout Scripture God gives us assurance that his promises for us are overflowing with good. In the previously quoted verse from Jeremiah 29:11 we see that God's heart toward us is to give us a hope and a future.

Jesus likewise speaks to us about the goodness of the Father: "Which of you, if your son asks for bread, will give him a stone? Or if he asks for a fish, will give him a snake? If you, then, though you are evil, know how to give good gifts to your children, how much more will your Father in heaven give good gifts to those who ask him" (Matthew 7:9–11).

What Jesus is communicating to us is that when we ask for something that is important in our hearts, our Heavenly Father doesn't just toss a rock at us, but he gives us soft, warm bread slathered in butter. His gifts are good because he is a good father.

These verses have significant personal meaning for my life.

Seven years after Gary's death, I drove to a local trail and went on a prayer walk to a river. I did this for forty-five days in a row.

Every day, I took with me a piece of homemade bread.

Every day, I brought my Bible and one ugly rock.

Day after day I ate a piece of delicious bread and I placed a rock in a pile on the edge of the river.

I read the verses out of the seventh chapter of Matthew. I prayed and meditated on God's desire to give me good bread instead of ugly rocks.

After forty-five days I left behind a pile of ugly rocks and carried with me memories of delicious bread, prayer, and the promises of God. Through this, God profoundly communicated to me his desire to provide good gifts to his children. My faith was strengthened, and my heart was filled with hope.

Because of this I am able to find joy in God's words to me about my destiny. Gary is a part of my story, but he is not the sum of it. As I pray according to God's plan and purpose, my Heavenly Father has good bread for me, and his plan will bring blessing and joy.

Prior to loss, like many others in my culture, I could breeze through life with bouncy optimism. I did not rely upon God's promises because, honestly, in my affluent self-sufficient country, I didn't need them.

In our culture we have our family, professions, homes, churches, vehicles, and beach vacations. We often don't need to seek the Lord to give us hope and a future.

But when we suffer, we are forced to our knees to a place of total dependence upon the Lord to give us a reason for living and the strength to press onward through our sorrow. It is at this place of desperation where God will pour out his spirit upon us and bless us with his words of delightful expectancy for our future.

The hope and vision for our future that God bestows upon us comes from a completely different source than those initial impulsive and illogical thoughts that we may have experienced during the early months of our bereavement.

True hope for our future is grounded in almighty God and his spirit flowing within us because his promises are solid and secure.

In Isaiah we read, "You will go out in joy and be led forth in peace; the mountains and hills will burst into song before you, and all the trees of the field will clap their hands" (Isaiah 55:12) .

And a few chapters later: "He (Jesus) will give a crown of beauty for ashes, a joyous blessing instead of mourning, festive praise instead of despair" (Isaiah 61:3 NLT).

And in Hebrews: "Let us hold unswervingly to the hope we profess, for he who promised is faithful" (Hebrews 10:23).

As we walk through loss, we must persevere in our grief and not run from it. When we have cried the tears that bereavement demands and when we have given expression to the lament in our hearts then we will be released from sadness and depression as a natural part of the process.

It's within the Lord's words of hope and assurance where will find the courage to walk through depression toward our future destiny of promise.

Ten

THE HOPE OF GRIEF

"But we do not want you to be uninformed, brothers, about
those who are asleep, that you may not grieve
as others do who have no hope."

1 Thessalonians 4:13 ESV

In the last chapter, we examined the common misconception that, if you have faith, you will not experience the depression associated with grieving.

Another common mistaken belief is the idea that, if you have hope that your loved one is in Heaven, you will not grieve the loss deeply or for a lengthy amount of time.

We live in a quick–fix culture where every problem is expected to have a solution before the end of the business day. As Americans, we believe that we are to get through our grief like an efficiently planned business meeting.

In the western world we value time above all else. We would more easily justify robbing a child of an ice cream sundae than interrupting a friend's schedule. Our lives are on the clock, and everything of value is measured in how many minutes are consumed. Busyness is a compelling status symbol. After all, success in our society is assessed by systematic production and speed. Powerful terms that are celebrated within our culture are:

- Keep going
- Press on
- Persist
- Be resolved
- Keep driving
- Stay the course

In our frenzied way of life, bereavement has been sterilized into a few orderly steps. The more rapidly a person advances through the list, the more we celebrate their progress.

In Latin America relationships are valued above professions and busyness. When I tried to set an appointment to have our pastor's family over for an afternoon meal, they looked at me as if it were ludicrous to turn people into an agenda.

The pastor's wife said to me in Spanish, "Why don't you just arrive at our home sometime and we'll enjoy a meal together."

My personality is naturally one of joyful spontaneity, but as an American I felt lost and confused with the casual approach to visiting a friend in Mexico. How could we just "show up" for a meal at their home? Why couldn't we set an appointment to spend an afternoon together?

Our professions, calendars on our phones, and crowded schedules are an essential element to personal identity in the States. It's no wonder that when loss comes knocking on our door, we set time–drive parameters much as we would a business meeting with a colleague.

There is nothing inherently wrong with our American values. There are many positive results derived from the national attributes I have mentioned. What is important to realize is how being an American affects our ability to process pain.

The characteristics that have made our country excel in business will cause ruin and dysfunction if applied to grief. We cannot have a broad response to every situation; we must apply grieving principles to bereavement and business standards to our professions.

Adding to our cultural tendency to avoid dealing with pain, Scripture instructs us to have hope. All through the Bible we read of the hope we have in Christ:

"The sufferings of this present time are not worth comparing with the glory that is to be revealed to us." (Romans 8:18 ESV)

"He will wipe away every tear from their eyes, and death shall be no more, neither shall there be mourning, nor crying, nor pain anymore, for the former things have passed away." (Revelation 21:4 ESV)

"He has caused us to be born again to a living hope through the resurrection of Jesus Christ from the dead, to an inheritance that is imperishable, undefiled, and unfading, kept in heaven for you." (1 Peter 1:3–4 ESV)

If we misunderstand these verses, we can develop the wrong idea that to grieve past a few months is to deny our hope in resurrection and restoration.

Or we can wrongly assume that if, because we have hope in heaven, that God will eliminate our earthly heartbreak and within a few months of the funeral we will experience carefree happiness.

When Gary died, my close widow and widower friends who had walked this journey before me explained that the second year after the loss of a spouse is more difficult than the first twelve months. I felt utter dismay at what they were saying and completely refused to acknowledge their words.

There was absolutely no way that I would allow the second year to be more painful than what I had already experienced.

I was determined to have hope. I assumed that if I continued my intense surge forward that, somehow, I would come out of this horrendous experience—quickly!—and with radiant optimism.

But if hope is not related to the speed of grief or a cheerful grin on our face, how *do* we mourn with hope?

I think we must embrace this truth: Grief and hope coexist. One does not replace the other.

As the scholar John Stott put it:

> We observe that Paul does not forbid us to grieve. Mourning is natural and emotionally necessary. It would be very unnatural, indeed inhuman, not to mourn when we lose somebody near and dear to us. To be sure, it is appropriate at Christian funerals joyfully to celebrate Christ's decisive victory over death, but we do so only through tears of personal sorrow. If Jesus wept at the graveside of his beloved friend Lazarus, his disciples are surely at liberty to do the same. What Paul prohibits is not grief but hopeless grief, not all mourning but mourning like the rest of men, who have no hope.[1]

Sometimes we forget that rather than grieving for our loved one who is joyfully worshipping their savior in heaven, we are grieving the loss of their presence in our day–to–day lives on earth. Yes, we have the

---

1   John Stott, *The Gospel & the End of Time: The Message of 1 & 2 Thessalonians* (Downers Grove, IL: Intervarsity Press, 1991).

assurance that we will one day be with them again in heaven, but it may be fifty years before we relax in Daddy's strong arms or feel the sweet kiss on our cheek from our little girl. The depth of our sorrow does not contradict our hope in Christ but instead shows the depth of the human relationship lost.

Often when I read Scripture, I imagine the story behind the narrative. The Biblical characters depicted were real flesh–and–blood people whose lives most certainly consisted of much more than the few sentences which we are given to read.

For example, in Luke we read of the man dying on the cross next to Jesus. He turned to Jesus and trusted that he was the Messiah. Jesus said to this man, "I assure you, today you will be with me in paradise" (Luke 23:43 NLT).

This was, indeed, a miraculous turn of events—and cause for celebration. But whoever was weeping at the foot of this man's cross was undoubtedly overwhelmed by the thought that her loved one would not be coming home that evening for a meal of fresh fish sizzling on an open fire.

Possibly his little sister may have heard Jesus' words of promise and comfort. But her big brother, who had taken care of their family, perhaps even stealing for their survival, would never come home again. She may have felt great hope that his years of thievery were forgiven and that he would spend eternity with the Messiah they had heard teach in the synagogue, but the earthly loss of her dear brother would be enormous, and for that she would agonize in grief.

The thread of hope in the midst of pain is woven throughout Tolkien's trilogy *The Lord of the Rings*. Tolkien does not avoid the deep pain of his characters, but neither does he leave us in despair nor overlook the power and grace of hope.

I feel the Fellowship's refusal to succumb to despair defies all logic. Inspired by their love for each other and their faith in the worthiness of their quest, they plod over mountains, brave blizzards, and flee armies of terrifying orcs, never abandoning their goal of reaching Mount Doom.

Gandalf explains the irony of their predicament: "That way lies our hope, where sits our greatest fear. Doom hangs still on a thread. Yet hope there is still, if we can but stand unconquered for a little while."

There is a beautiful amalgamation between our ability to feel sorrow deeply at the same moment we walk in profound hope.

Three years into my trek as a widow, Bethany, who is a talented artist, gave me a drawing of Samwise Gamgee and Rosie Cotton on their wedding day. She knew that I related closely with Frodo, who never healed from his suffering and sailed away to the Undying Lands. Bethany wanted to instill within me the promise of Sam and Rosie, who were able to transcend loss and bask in the delights of marriage.

She wanted to give me hope.

Hope in the midst of grief is a paradox. It sounds impossible, but it is quite possible. And here's why. We read in Thessalonians that *grieving with hope* is not only possible, but we are instructed to do it: "But we do not want you to be uninformed, brothers, about those who are asleep, that you may not grieve others do who have no hope" (1 Thessalonians 4:13 ESV).

We mistakenly think that the opposite of hope is grief.

The truth is that the opposite of hope is despair.

In other words, while hope does not displace grief, it certainly can eliminate despair.

I have a vivid memory of what despair looks like.

My grandfather died at a young age while working on a roof for a friend. I was seven years old at the time, and my family and I were camping in the mountains of western Pennsylvania. The park ranger came to our location in the forest and told my dad that there was an emergency at home.

In this pre-cellphone era I recollect my dad's face when he stood in the tiny supply store at the pay phone talking with his sister. And looking back with the mind of a small child I remember being disappointed that our long–awaited summer vacation was cut short.

But the most vivid image from that tragedy that has stuck in my mind for all these years is that of my grandmother at the funeral. At one point during the service she ran up to the coffin and began grabbing at my grandfather's body and screaming. This shocked everyone, especially the young children present. A few male relatives pried her away from his body and into a private room where we still heard her screams reverberating throughout the dimly lit building.

Sadly, my grandma had no hope. She did not know about her beloved's life in heaven with Jesus. She did not have the message or peace of salvation. All she knew was the wretched loss of her husband without any hope that he was at peace or that she would see him again.

What my grandma didn't have was the gift of hope in her heart. The promise of our loved one residing with Jesus in heaven is a gift given to us within the anguish so that even though we are in great pain, we need not despair.

When Scripture tells us to grieve with hope it is not meant to scold or correct, but to encourage. The Apostle Paul shared with believers the truth of the resurrection and heaven to give them a refuge from despair that the world around them did not have. He was not scolding them like a grumpy uncle, instead he was giving believers the gift of confidence in resurrection life for our loved ones who have died.

In Mexico, as Nathaniel, Bethany, and I said goodbye to Gary's body, I took his hand and will never forget the icy cold of death. His fingers felt frozen and lifeless, and I knew my husband was in heaven. His precious body lay on the couch, the man I'd known intimately for the eighteen years of marriage was no longer there.

In that moment, my children and I didn't rejoice but we also didn't despair. We calmly got up off our knees and walked into the kitchen knowing the next time we saw my husband and their daddy we would be standing next to him in heaven.

I often feel amazed at God's grace of hope upon my life. I am frequently stopped on the street by people who compliment the depth of my joy and the expanse of my smile.

One man approached me in Macy's and said, "You have a beautiful smile. Thank you for sharing it."

When I hear these genuine compliments, I am stunned. Part of me would like to invite these people to a worship service right in the middle of the athletic shoe department. I want to say, "Do you know what I have been through? Can you comprehend all that God has done in my heart?"

There is no human explanation for the radiance that God has given to me. It is only by God's grace and mercy that I am alive let alone walking in the glory of his hope and joy.

God promises to renew our strength. We will not be overcome with despair in our journey of grief and sorrow.

"Those who hope in the Lord
    will renew their strength.
They will soar on wings like eagles;
    they will run and not grow weary,
    they will walk and not be faint." (Isaiah 40:31 NIV)

Hope, therefore, is a sacred and precious gift from God. When we realize that hope is something we can experience even in the depth of our pain, our hearts can't help but overflow with worship for Jesus and all that he has done.

Nathaniel, Gary, and Bethany after a long day of work on the house.

The renovated building where love and ministry flowed from Gary and Rachel's lives.
The green gate is where they met on a sunny afternoon and went into town for a
romantic saunter through the cobblestone streets of Taxco.

A family hike where Gary, Rachel, Nathaniel, and Bethany discovered tropical plants, flowers, and Aztec ruins.

Gary chatting with Silvia. Oscar and Silvia were the family's first friends in Taxco.

*Gary and Oscar talking about the Bible after the two families enjoyed a
delicious meal prepared by Silvia.*

Gary and Rachel

Their last family photo together:
Gary, Rachel, Bethany, and Nathaniel in Mexico as missionaries.

Gary and Rachel's renovated home and ministry center in southern Mexico. They were sitting on the stairs listening to the motmot bird when Gary experienced the heart attack that killed him.

From left to right: Bethany, Nathaniel, Rachel,
and Nathaniel's wife, Dorie, in Chicago, 2020.

Rachel in Colorado six years after Gary's death.

Eleven

THE EMPTINESS OF GRIEF

"The Lord your God is in your midst, a mighty one who will save; he will rejoice over you with gladness; he will quiet you by his love; he will exult over you with loud singing."

Zephaniah 3:17 ESV

Predawn darkness fills the kitchen as a three-year-old boy stumbles into the room with sleepy eyes.

"Mama, come play with me," he cries as his eyes fill with tears, but there is no one there to answer. He peers into the dark and empty room. "Where is Mama? Gramma, where is Mama?"

The grief-worn woman comes to him and holds her grandson close, but he is inconsolable.

His gramma is kind and her snuggly sweatshirt smells of last evening's cookie dough, but right now the little boy only wants his mama. He cries for the familiar fragrance of her perfume and to nestle in her arms.

"Mama, Mama!" he sobs not understanding why she will not come to him.

Gramma is comforting, kind, and loving, but she cannot replace this little boy's mama.

Amie gazes at her mom's dresser where the perfume and jewelry have remained untouched for the past two years.

"You promised to show me how to wear makeup when I turned thirteen, but you lied!" she cries out, and as soon as the words fall off her lips she feels a horrible sense of shame and guilt. How awful for her to speak these terrible and untrue things about her mom.

She knows cancer stole her mother from her, but what she *feels* is abandonment—and she can't get rid of the haunting thought that if she had just been pretty enough or smart enough her mom wouldn't have gone away.

Suddenly she hears the front door open. She shudders as she hears two voices—her dad's, and the higher-pitched voice of a woman.

"She's here," Amie moans, feeling the sudden urge to flee.

"Sweetheart!" her father calls up the stairs. "Lisa's here—she has a present for you! Some perfume!"

Amie feels nauseated at the thought of facing her dad's new girlfriend. Her eyes fill with tears. "I hate her. She is nice and all, but I feel like she is an intruder trying to be my mom."

William needs to be in his home office in ten minutes for an online meeting. He has just enough time to head toward the kitchen to grab a cup of coffee. The problem is that he must pass the nursery before he is able to reach the coffee pot.

As he does, he sees his wife sitting in the glider next to the empty crib, staring at Emma's blankets and the brightly colored stuffed animals. In an odd way, seeing her just staring blankly is a relief, as he remembers the day last week when he found her inside the crib, curled into a ball and sobbing.

"Honey, are you okay?" he asks.

"Yeah, I'm doing better today than I was last week. But my mom called again."

William winced.

"She's still asking when we're going to start trying to have another baby." Grace leans over and reaches for a tissue. "I remember holding little Emma as her tiny fingers wrapped around mine. She was perfect, ya know, everything about her was beautiful. She was just so small. . ."

"What did you say to your mom?" He tries to hide his frustration.

"I told her to please stop asking me about another baby. I told her we're not ready. As if another baby could replace little Emma as if she never existed."

After the death of a loved one, there is a "vacancy" sign on our soul, but does that mean another mama, wife, or baby should check in so that the vacancy is filled? Death leaves us isolated and alone with a deep longing for the person we have lost—and yet there is no replacement on earth for what we are truly missing.

This is not a difficult concept for us to grasp, at least not when we really stop and think about it. Granted, when someone we love is grieving, in our desperation to help we can say dumb things (or at least think them even if we know better than to put them into words).

"This new baby will help you forget the one who died."

"I know your spouse just died, but you'll feel better once you start dating again."

"I know you miss your dad, but when your mom remarries, you'll have a new dad!"

In fact, we are not above falling into this kind of thinking even when we are the one who is bereaved.

Five years into my grief when I began to date a respected and godly man in my church, I had idealistic and innocent ideas that a new husband would repair the devastation that death had brought into my life. I already knew the delights of marriage and how wonderful our world can be. As a widowed woman falling in love, I imagined whimsical scenes of a new joy–filled life for my children and me.

My children didn't share my optimism.

I was puzzled by their lack of enthusiasm. One evening before an anticipated date with this handsome man who I admired and loved deeply, I said to Bethany, "Don't you want another dad?"

She looked at me with ice in her blue eye. "I do not want a substitute! Once you've had a wonderful dad and he has died, there is no way to desire someone to take his place."

The desire for a father is strong and undeniable and never goes away—but for my children, the person of "Dad" is gone forever. While, of course, both of my children would love a father in their life, there's no way to go back and recreate the past and make someone who wasn't their daddy into him now. Nathaniel and Bethany long for a father's love and the close relationship that they shared with Gary, but as adults the only father that either one of them will ever know has been burned to ashes and buried under a lemon tree in southern Mexico.

Every grieving person's desire is to be with the loved one who was destroyed by death. They don't want to go shopping for a replacement, as if they could go to Macy's or Kohl's and replace their loved one like last year's athletic shoes or swimsuit.

Benevolent children may welcome "Mom's new husband" or "Dad's new wife" into their lives, but that person will never become Daddy or Mama to them.

Likewise, when a widow or widower gets remarried, the new spouse will never take the place of the previous one. The two relationships are distinctly deep and profound connections at separate times in a man or woman's life.

We may enjoy a new and incredible relationship, but it will never occupy the same corner of our heart that will forever belong to the person who has died.

Relationships cannot be replaced; they must be grieved.

And when we really stop to think about it, we know this is true.

But there is a "replacement theory" that is more insidious and harder to combat. We've probably all said it to someone who is grieving. And if we've grieved a horrendous loss, we've undoubtedly heard it from well-meaning friends and loved ones.

We believe these words. And if we don't experience them in real life like we think we should, we still believe them—and feel flawed or guilty that we can't seem to feel the comfort we think they should provide.

What is the replacement theory we are told and that we tell ourselves and others?

That God can be the replacement that fills the void that our loved one left.

Pastors and church counselors repeatedly tried to encourage me with the idea that, while Gary had been burned to ashes, I should look on the bright side because Jesus would be my husband now.

I know in their hearts they meant well, and if we don't think too deeply about it, this can sound like a rather impressive exchange.

My husband was a flawed human man, and in exchange I would receive a perfect, loving, and sacrificial savior. Wow, on the surface it can sound amazing!

But if truth be told, these words pierced my heart deeply and made my skin crawl. I was bereft of my husband, but now I was also expected to be married to God himself?

Lying in my widow's bed, I laid my hand on Gary's pillow and looked at his untouched blankets. In that moment, I felt the absurdity of the idea that Jesus would be my surrogate husband, and it didn't take much critical thinking to know that the counsel I had received must certainly be wrong.

I began to ask these questions and many more.

- Would Jesus teach Nathaniel and Bethany math as Gary had done?
- Would Jesus provide a monthly income as Gary had done?
- Would Jesus show Nathaniel how to shave?
- Would Jesus walk Bethany down the aisle?
- Would Jesus play Nerf guns or an intense game of chess with my children?
- Would Jesus tickle Bethany and snuggle her in his arms?
- Would Jesus take out the trash, empty the dishwasher, or paint my kitchen?
- Would Jesus garden with me? Would he pull weeds when I am tired, or lift sod to add another flower bed?
- Would Jesus run to the store for me when I'm elbow deep in cake flour and forgot to purchase vanilla?
- Would Jesus tell me I was pretty and look at me with desire?
- Would Jesus snuggle me in the morning or make love to me at night?

When well-meaning friends or counselors tell us "Just tuck into Jesus. He will be your husband now," we need think through their words in a logical and theological fashion.

God promises to be the father to the fatherless and a husband to the widow but is Scripture saying that he is literally a replacement to these treasured earthly relationships? Does Scripture *really* promise us that Jesus will be a widow's next husband or a widower's new wife? Does a young man, who buried his beautiful twenty-year-old bride, stand at the counter marked *exchanges only*, truly believing that Jesus will show up, purple luggage in hand, ready to be his wife?

These are ludicrous ideas that we must refute with Scripture as well as a good dose of logic.

In the story of creation in Genesis, God says to Adam, "It is not good for man to be alone." The God of all knew that Adam should not be left alone with only the trinity for companionship and procreation.

Therefore, we must accept the truth that God himself views human relationships as valuable, and when lost they cannot be replaced by his own presence.

So where do we get this misunderstanding about God's intentions of replacing human spouses?

In Isaiah we read, "Do not be afraid; you will not be put to shame. Do not fear disgrace; you will not be humiliated. You will forget the shame of your youth and remember no more the reproach of your widowhood. For your Maker is your husband—the LORD Almighty is his name—the Holy One of Israel is your Redeemer; he is called the God of all the earth" (Isaiah 54:4–5).

When we read this passage, it is important to understand to whom God is speaking. This is a beautiful section of Scripture where we read of God's love and protection for Israel as they are being taken into captivity in hostile Babylon. The Babylonian exile meant more than oppression and servitude for Israel; it meant shame, disgrace, and humiliation. Their slavery is compared to widowhood, not because men and women were literally without their spouses but because of the shame and reproach the nation of Israel experienced in their captivity to Babylon.

God promised to be a husband to Israel while his people were in slavery—not to those who have been bereaved.

We cannot pick a verse of Scripture and proclaim it as truth for those who grieve when this passage is not talking about death but captivity.

However, we must concede that throughout the Bible the narrative is abundant with the characterization of God who defends and cares for us:

- He is our protection.
- He is our provider.
- He is love.
- He is wisdom.
- He is our redeemer.
- He is faithful.

All these attributes show that God is profoundly faithful and infinitely loving to his people.

However, when a beloved wife dies, when an honored father is buried, when parents carry a small casket to a grave site, *Jesus cannot and is not supposed to be* a replacement for earthly relationships lost.

Gary and Jesus are two distinct beings—*neither is a stand-in for the other.*

Jesus isn't my husband, and Gary wasn't my savior.

We cannot attempt to replace people, even if we are trying to find the replacement in the arms of God.

So what does God want to give us? What is his commitment to widows, widowers, and children without a parent?

What God can provide to us is profound and of immeasurable value. After all, the Holy Spirt is called our "comforter," and Abba Father promises to walk with each one of us in our grief.

As we journey through loss, our depth of faith is an essential component of healing our sorrow. The intimacy that we share with the lover of our soul is deep and profound. We can trust him to walk alongside us on our pilgrimage through grief and sorrow as he quiets us with his love.

The psalmist says, "The Lord is close to the broken hearted and saves those who are crushed in spirit" (Psalm 34:18).

And Jesus says, "Blessed are those who mourn, for they will be comforted" (Matthew 5:4).

However, in the early years of bereavement, sorrow has a way of alienating us from every aspect of who we are, and that includes a type of spiritual estrangement.

Early in our grief, Nathaniel, Bethany, and I would gather in our living room attempting to continue the tradition of family worship and devotions. But picking up our Bibles to read Scripture—and hearing the echoes of Gary's voice—became too much to endure.

We would end up quietly walking away and retreating to isolated places of sorrow. We were unable to bear the pain of engaging in beloved spiritual disciplines without our cherished dad and husband.

When he was in the Desert of Judah, David wrote, "O God, you are my God; earnestly I seek you; my soul thirsts for you; my flesh faints for you, as in a dry and weary land where there is no water" (Psalm 63:1).

But what happens when we are not able to seek him earnestly or even walk to the stream where he promises living water?

Henri Nouwen writes, "The friend who can be silent with us in a moment of despair or confusion, who can stay with us in an hour of grief and bereavement, who can tolerate not knowing. . . not healing, not curing. . . that is a friend who cares."

The greatest ministry that other believers were able to do for my children and me was to carry us to the feet of Jesus. We were broken and paralyzed in our pain. Our spiritual feet could not walk.

In Luke 5, the story of the paralyzed man being lowered down through the roof while Jesus was teaching tells us:

"One day Jesus was teaching, and Pharisees and teachers of the law were sitting there. They had come from every village of Galilee and from Judea and Jerusalem. And the power of the Lord was with Jesus to heal the sick. Some men came carrying a paralyzed man on a mat and tried to take him into the house to lay him before Jesus. When they could not find a way to do this because of the crowd, they went up on the roof and lowered him on his mat through the tiles into the middle of the crowd, right in front of Jesus" (Luke 5: 17-19).

In this Biblical narrative we see loving and faithful men who carried their friend to Jesus and even made a hole in the roof in order to be certain that the Lord saw and healed him.

This passage of Scripture is profound. What kind of men cared enough to break through the ceiling of a building to get their friend to Jesus? They were men who realized that their friend could not get to the Messiah on his own. Therefore, they used their strength, time, and effort to bring him into the presence of God.

This is an important message for us as the body of Christ. What kind of friends are we? Are we the type of companions who bear the burden of the hurting ones and take them into God's presence even if it means making radical decisions and ruining a few roofs?

Or are we part of the crowd who would pat a paralyzed man on the back and say, "Brother, just tuck into Jesus," as we go on our way walking joyfully down the road?

Our friends who have gone through devastating loss need us to carry them. Jesus does not want them to crawl on bloody knees on their own. God does not want the grieving ones to be so drastically alone that they must dig a hole in the roof in order to find Jesus all by themselves.

My friend Kim told me about a time she found herself in the carnage of sorrow and loss. Despite growing up in a charismatic church, in her pain, God felt far away. In fact, she'd stopped going to church months before.

One day Kim's best friend Shelley—who didn't share her charismatic background—called and said, "Kim, what you need is to get to a place where your heart connects with God. I know you love the worship center at the church downtown. And I'm taking you there. I will pick you up at 7:00."

"The worship center? All last year I invited you to go with me. You said you'd never step a foot inside." Kim managed a smile.

"I'll pick you up in an hour!"

Shelley, who came from a liturgical background, set aside her own apprehension and—quite literally!—brought Kim to the feet of Jesus in the way that she needed. This act of sacrifice renewed Kim's hurting heart and gave her the courage to begin the healing process after loss.

Jesus longs for his children to gather around people who have been catapulted into a pit of sorrow. Shelley was able to do that for Kim. I'm sure it wasn't easy for her as someone accustomed to strict liturgy to walk into a charismatic worship center. But she knew that her friend needed to connect with God in a way that felt familiar to her. And through her act of sacrifice she was able to help Kim find her way.

Another example of bringing someone to the feet of Jesus happened to me during Nathaniel's high school graduation.

It was only three years after Gary's death, and I knew that I would be surrounded by hundreds of moms and dads honoring their graduates.

I was completely grief-stricken at the thought of walking up on stage with the many fully intact homeschool couples after the painful annihilation of my once unbroken family. I feared standing completely alone giving my tribute to Nathaniel, as I was the only single parent in this traditional homeschool group.

My dear friend Andrea did not ask me what I needed her to do. She did not offer pat answers. She did not insist that I suck it up and smile.

During the two–hour ceremony, she simply sat next to me and prayed and held my hand. She did not focus on her own comfort or her own pressing schedule with her family. She just sat beside me holding my hand and praying me through this very painful time.

Somehow the pain of walking on stage alone was lessened because Andrea was with me. God used Andrea's willingness to just *be* with me to lessen my pain and bring me to the feet of Jesus.

We are to bring those who are in devastating pain into his presence. When we lay down our fear and the preservation of our level of comfort, we can bring deep healing into the lives of our friends and loved ones.

What we see in Scripture is that God's grace covers us with his comfort and love. When we are thrown headfirst into bereavement, we may feel a sense of condemnation for not being able to seek the Lord as we once did. But God's heart is turned toward his beloved children and his grace carries us when we do not have the ability to walk to him on our own.

In Isaiah we read, "Like a shepherd He will tend His flock, in His arm He will gather the lambs and carry them in His bosom; He will gently lead the nursing ewes" (Isaiah 40:11 NASB).

Our Good Shepherd holds us in the very palm of his nail–pierced hand, and we are very precious to him. He is our beloved savior, friend, and intimate comfort.

Jesus will never be a replacement wife to a grieving widowed husband, or a replacement child for a parent grieving the loss of a cherished little girl. But because he loves us more than we can imagine we can rest in him. He embraces us with his presence, and we can be confident that God, who began the good work in us, will in his grace take us where he wants us to be.

Twelve

THE DANCE OF GRIEF

"You turned my wailing into dancing; you removed my
sackcloth and clothed me with joy, that my heart may sing
your praises and not be silent. Lord my God,
I will praise you forever"

Psalm 30:11

It was our tenth wedding anniversary and Gary walked down the stairs in our home. He wore his handsome tweed jacket and turned on the soft jazz. My red dress flowed gracefully as he took my hand and twirled me to the music.

Having spent years in Mexico, few things bring me as much joy as the beautiful flow of Latino dance. There's deep expression and meaning with every passionate movement and step.

However, not every dance is so beautiful. A few years ago, when I slammed my toe into our metal coffee table there was absolutely no joy or beauty in *that* dance. My foot swelled up and turned an ugly black and blue. I wore a bulky athletic shoe two sizes too large and stumbled through my days wincing in pain. And even if I had tried some beautiful Latino dance steps at that point, I don't believe the most lovestruck man could have seen beauty in my clumsy movements when my toe was broken.

When Gary died, I felt as if I could not breathe from the suffocating weight of suffering. I felt physically, emotionally, and spiritually crushed and broken from the intensity of pain. The psalmist writes about God turning wailing into dancing, but can God honestly expect us to dance even with a mangled leg, broken toe? And what about a shattered heart?

And is this dance that he gives us a thing of beauty or brokenness?

The Lord of the Rings has become a sacred family story whether through the written word of Tolkien or Peter Jackson's epic rendition on the screen. What hits me deeply every time I read or watch this story is the theme of brokenness and suffering.

When the members of the Fellowship return home from their treacherous mission, the haunting experiences of their heartbreaking—but victorious—journey remained with them.

Yet, the adversity of their travels forged in each member of the Fellowship tremendous courage and depth.

We see this particularly with the character of Frodo Baggins.

Imagine with me if Frodo hadn't been chosen to take the ring to Mordor. What would his life have looked like as a carefree young man of the Shire? Would he have achieved the depth of character and wisdom that were wrought in him through his journey?

Would we prefer to trade shallow chitchat over a beer with a jovial Frodo, or find ourselves captivated by every word from this valiant and heroic hobbit who faced the very fires of Mordor?

Here's another example. Let us consider J.R.R. Tolkien himself.

By the time Tolkien was the tender age of twelve, both of his parents had died. As a young man, he walked alone into the blistering wilderness of war.

He later wrote to his son Christopher, "If anguish were visible, almost the whole of this benighted planet would be enveloped in a dense dark vapor, shrouded from the amazed vision of the heavens!"

From his writings, it would appear that the soul of young Tolkien was in turmoil as World War I consumed the lives around him. However, in the midst of these dark, challenging times, he was driven onward writing his manuscripts from the trenches of battle, where he carried out God's great purpose.

Frodo speaks from Tolkien's pen. "How do you pick up the threads of an old life? How do you go on, when in your heart you begin to understand. . . there is no going back? There are some things that time cannot mend. Some hurts that go too deep, that have taken hold."

Because of the loss of his parents and the death of his closest friends, we can speculate that Tolkien bore the emotional scars of sorrow and loss for the rest of his life. If Tolkien had not suffered great loss, would *The Lord of the Rings* have even been written? And even if it had, could it have espoused the depth of insights into suffering—and overcoming—that we see in these beloved characters?

Despite Tolkien's losses—*or more importantly because of them*—he was able to create the greatest epic narrative of our time.

I am fascinated by stories of people who have survived suffering and gone on to see their wailing turned into dancing—even if their dance contained a painful limp.

Take, for example, this story about Jacob, told in Genesis 32:

So Jacob was left alone, and a man wrestled with him till daybreak. When the man saw that he could not overpower him, he touched the socket of Jacob's hip so that his hip was wrenched as he wrestled with the man. Then the man said, "Let me go, for it is daybreak."

But Jacob replied, "I will not let you go unless you bless me."

The man asked him, "What is your name?"

"Jacob," he answered.

Then the man said, "Your name will no longer be Jacob, but Israel, because you have struggled with God and with humans and have overcome."

Jacob said, "Please tell me your name."

But he replied, "Why do you ask my name?" Then he blessed him there.

So Jacob called the place Peniel, saying, "It is because I saw God face to face, and yet my life was spared."

The sun rose above him as he passed Peniel, and he was limping because of his hip. (Genesis 32:24–31)

There's something profound in this Biblical narrative. When Jacob wrestled with the Angel of the Lord, this experience resulted in both a painful limp and a blessing.

God honored Jacob and called him Israel, entrusting him with an eventual nation of people, a community that represented God's own name.

Yet, for the rest of his life Jacob was reminded of the night that he battled with God in prayer, as he endured the pain from a hip that was forever out of joint.

Let's be honest, this truth is uncomfortable for all of us. After all, who loves the concepts of wounds, brokenness, and limps? No one.

The Bible doesn't tell us how Jacob's bride, Rachel, reacted to her husband's deformity. But grant me some creative license as my imagination interprets this familiar story.

We already know that the Jewish culture is full of exuberance and celebration. I can imagine that Jacob, now named Israel by the voice of God, danced at his sons' weddings. Did he take Rachel's hand and move his feet to the Horah? For his beautiful wife, what was it like to be married to a man who had a deformed hip?

In my imagination I hear Rachel saying, "Please, honey, when you dance with me at Benjamin's wedding leave that ugly shepherd's cane with Leah."

I'm assuming that Rachel wanted to be a woman of depth and godly character. At the same time, she may not have relished the idea of taking the hand of a man who awkwardly danced with a limp.

Likewise, you and I may find ourselves desiring significance and inner beauty, while hoping to avoid the suffering that refines us.

We want Jacob's blessing but not Jacob's limp.

We want to believe being fully human means transcending pain and loss without any disfigurement. But I would contend to be fully human is to be broken and refined by suffering.

We are created in the image of God and because of the perfection of creation we naturally appreciate and enjoy things of unbroken beauty.

As a result, our desire for wholeness is seen in the profound as well as the simple or mundane. One of my favorite things, even as an adult, is a brand-new giant box of Crayola crayons. When my children were young, I bought them new crayons frequently even when there were plenty of broken pieces lying around. I have always delighted in the fresh fragrance and the beauty of the colors lined up in a tidy unspoiled row.

Broken crayons are ugly, and they're harder to use with their stubby tops and crumbling paper. I don't think anyone would choose a broken crayon over a fresh new one that is ready to create artistic design.

In light of this, I recently saw a social media post that stated, "God still uses broken crayons."

While I appreciate the sentiment, I have to take issue with what it is implying. By using the word "still," the statement seems to suggest that God looks at our condition and says, "Well, I see that you are a broken, ugly, torn, and stubby crayon but I'll find a way to use you anyway."

No way!

I believe that God looks at our brokenness, not as a discarded crayon, but as a thing of priceless beauty and value. Peter agreed when writing, "So that the proof of your faith, being more precious than gold which is perishable, even though tested by fire, may be found to result in praise and glory and honor at the revelation of Jesus Christ" (2 Peter 1:7 NASB).

Paul confirms this idea when he writes, "But we have this treasure in jars of clay, to show that the surpassing power belongs to God and not to us. We are afflicted in every way, but not crushed; perplexed, but not driven to despair; persecuted, but not forsaken; struck down, but not destroyed; always carrying in the body the death of Jesus, so that the life of Jesus may also be manifested in our bodies. For we who live are always being given over to death for Jesus' sake, so that the life of Jesus also may be manifested in our mortal flesh" (2 Corinthians 4:7–11 ESV).

So what does it look like for me to dance with the limp of grief and trauma? Does it mean I am mangled and ruined? Will I be destined forever to be the broken box of crayons discarded in the corner of the playroom? Something that God uses reluctantly when there are not more "whole" people available to Him?

Will sorrow and loss prevent me from the graceful dance that I once knew?

Does God come to our broken–up box of crayons and with a halfhearted fatherly resolve say, "Yeah, I suppose I can color with this."

Never!

Instead, God says, "My child, I actually *can't* use you unless you are broken. The process may hurt like hell, but I will be with you every step of your journey. And even when I am silent and you cannot sense my presence, I will be with you. In the end you will be a priceless diamond that will shine forth my glory, but it is only possible through the suffering that you must go through."

Paul breaks down the value of brokenness when he writes, "But he said to me, "My grace is sufficient for you, for my power is made perfect in weakness." Therefore, I will boast all the more gladly about my weaknesses, so that Christ's power may rest on me" (2 Corinthians 12:9).

I have discovered that we who have suffered are pure gold. We who have endured catastrophic losses are sparkling diamonds! The Lord not only delights in using us when our life has collapsed, brokenness is the pathway to blessing and being used profoundly by the hand of God.

I have experienced much pain throughout my life, and yet there is also fathomless joy.

How do I reconcile these two seemingly mutually exclusive life experiences?

I have discovered that leaning into suffering creates a deeper sense of rejoicing. If I incline myself toward the sadness, I can experience everything within my surroundings in a richer, more penetrating way. My heart and feelings have not been dulled by the ordinary, rather they are made alive through sorrow and loss. My senses grasp the intricacies of the depths of human emotion.

And in the process, my suffering becomes the catalyst for pleasure and gratitude.

When we go through catastrophic loss, in desperation we hasten to make our suffering cease and our sorrow disappear. However, there is a beautiful and graceful way to dance with the pain while living a life of blessing and abundant joy.

When we fight against our pain, we become exhausted, bitter, angry, and miserable. And when we wallow in our pain, we become morose, depressed, sullen, and dismal.

Conversely, when we accept this partnership of pain in our life, like Jacob, we will come to a place of blessing and joy.

Nothing we do, from the day of horrific loss onward, will take grief away from us. So it is necessary to lean into him, ask what he desires to teach us, and look for the blessings he will bestow upon our lives.

There are many rich and precious things that are part of the legacy of grief. But first we must take off our boxing gloves and learn to see grief as a holy avenue of grace, blessing, and intensity of love.

Because of the legacy that sorrow has given to me my life has been enriched in various ways:

- I am empowered to admire and honor a man in a way that I never understood before. I deeply loved Gary, but it has only been through his death that the grace of respect for the men in my life radiates from my very being. What I once struggled with and found awkward and burdensome now flows freely from my heart. This is only one of many of the graces that have been poured upon me within the sorrow of my husband's death.

- I have been passionate about the beauty of the written word for many years. Yet my manuscripts lacked depth and were insipid imitations of other authors' works. However, watching my husband die on the Mexican pavement has given me the ability to write from my heart and reach into the depths of others' lives with my words.

- Prayer is the foundation that Gary's and my marriage was built upon, and it has been a lasting spiritual legacy in our family. With grief as my constant companion I am able to pray for people whose lives have fallen apart, and there is an anointing upon me that I did not work to obtain. It is a gift of the Holy Spirit and a grace given to me because of the outpouring of suffering.

All these things and many more like them have been bestowed upon me *because of my journey of grief—not in spite of it!*

Those of us who walk the journey of grief have a way of dancing that is different from most. It's unlike anything others have experienced. It's not hip-hop. It's not swing. It's not ball room. And it's not even Latin.

Counterintuitively, when we walk the journey of grief the beauty of dancing with a limp is valuable beyond measure. It is a splendid two-step reserved for those who bear the scars of grief. It's one of the most graceful dances you will ever witness, but it is not something you are able to take a class and learn. It is a waltz that you must experience firsthand.

When we learn to live with grief as our companion, we experience a beauty and anointing that we have never known before. When we dance with a limp, our savior carries us and lifts our feet along the floor and makes the steps of our life beautiful and graceful before him.

Anne Lamott writes, "You will lose someone you can't live without, and your heart will be badly broken, and the bad news is that you never completely get over the loss of your beloved. But this is also the good news. They live forever in your broken heart that doesn't seal back up. And you come through. It's like having a broken leg that never heals perfectly—that still hurts when the weather gets cold, but you learn to dance with the limp."[2]

---

2   Anne Lamott, *Plan B: Further Thoughts on Faith* (New York: Penguin Books USA, 2005).

Thirteen

THE LOSSES OF GRIEF

"To provide for those who grieve in Zion, to give them a crown of beauty instead of ashes, the oil of joy for mourning, and a garment of praise in place of a spirit of despair..."

Isaiah 61:3

"O Holy Night" played triumphantly from the radio station KDKA out of Pittsburgh, but my most beloved Christmas song felt hollow. It was 1977 and my grandma had moved into my parents' modest split entry home. Her bedroom was across from mine, and oftentimes I heard her softly crying as she struggled for each life–giving breath.

One morning an ambulance took my grandma away because she couldn't breathe, and I ran into her room and grasped the pretty purple nightgown she had worn as gut–wrenching sobs filled my body. She died of congestive heart failure on a cold Pennsylvania morning in January only one day after we had celebrated New Year's together.

At twelve years old, I found it burdensome to go through the adult ritual of a funeral and the subsequent lunch in the church basement. I wanted to be left alone. I didn't desire to spend the afternoon eating sandwiches with a bunch of distant relatives and listening to them talk about my grandma as if they had known her in the way that I had.

Shortly after my grandma's death, her room in our home was transformed back to what it had been, and the days turned into weeks and then months.

Despite my sorrow, life went on as usual.

I maintained the same routine at school. My best friend Marci and I continued giggling about the boys that we liked. I struggled in math and excelled in creative writing. I watched the same shows after school on TV and played the same board games with my sister. My dad's job at the steel mill remained as it always had been, and my mom continued to make the best pot roast in all of western Pennsylvania!

My family felt the loss of the relationship with my grandma, but our lives were untouched by lasting upheaval.

This is the normative experience when our elderly family members die full of years and ready to journey to heaven.

But when untimely death knocks on a family's private door, we can experience losses that go beyond longing for the person who has died. Our world has turned upside down and inside out and suddenly most everything in our life has changed or disappeared.

Bereavement does not create a single hole; instead it impacts nearly every area of our life. There is a domino effect called secondary losses. The first domino is the loss of the person, but the second is knocked over because the first one fell. And row upon row, the pieces of our life come crashing down upon each other.

In my own story, after the initial shock wore off, I began to see the extensive devastation that Gary's death had caused. As I stumbled around trying to make sense of everything that had been stripped away from my life, I felt vulnerable and robbed of dignity, as if someone had torn off my clothes and raped me.

Everyone's secondary losses are different, but here are a few of the most significant ones that ravaged my life:

1. I lost my husband and dearest friend.

Gary and I enjoyed a deep and cherished friendship throughout our marriage. We spent many hours on our backyard swing among the flower gardens sharing about our life together and our personal hopes and visions for our future. We were each other's absolute best friend and never wanted to do things apart. We shared everything from the depths of prayer to the most jovial banter. The sudden disappearance of my best and dearest friend created a vast deficiency in my life.

2. I lost sexual intimacy.

Sexual intimacy within marriage brings delightful lightheartedness, and I believe it is a gift given by God as a grown-up form of playfulness. Sex is not only the intimate connection as a couple but also a place where we are able to be whimsical and free-spirited, absent from worry and responsibility. We also have an intense drive for physical connection. Sexual fulfillment within marriage is a part of our identity as adults. As humans we were created as male and female given to each other within the sanctity of marriage. Therefore, the banishment of our sexuality and sexual expression is an enormous void for the widow and widower.

3. I lost our ministry.

When Gary and I married we spent hours talking about the things of God and our desire to serve him together in ministry. We moved in tandem as equal partners with different but complementary spiritual gifts. Eventually, we founded a nonprofit organization, Swordmaster Ministries Inc., which was the reason we were ministering in Mexico when Gary died. Our goal was to train Mexican nationals to become mature pastors and give them the tools they needed to lead scripturally saturated and culturally effective churches throughout Latin America.

Swordmaster Ministries Inc. would not have existed without Gary, and it would not have been the same organization without me. I could not pick up the pieces after his death and carry on with the work that we had begun together. God called us to be missionaries together, and the ministry could not continue when one of us was gone. The impact of the elimination of our ministry was an incomprehensible loss that I experienced in addition to losing Gary as my husband.

4. I lost my profession and my source of income.

Throughout our marriage Gary and I were in church leadership in various capacities. During those years he continued a career in computer-based training, design, and writing. When we established Swordmaster Ministries Inc. he resigned from his position at USDA in northern Colorado, and we relied upon our ministry partners for income on the mission field in Mexico. When Gary died, my life as a missionary—*and my income*—ended. While I have rebuilt a career in real estate, the financial repercussions of the loss of income after Gary's death have followed me for years.

5. I lost my beautiful home.

As a real estate agent, I occasionally sell a home because of death or divorce but most often the changing of an address is a joyful celebration.

Recently, a client surprised me with a question about my own personal dream home. Because of my profession, I explore and show many beautiful Colorado properties, so the question of what style and configuration suits me would seem like an easy question to answer. But for some reason I stumbled around, unsure of what to say.

The next day it dawned on me that I'd been unable to answer because my dream home lies in the barrio de Casallas and not in the local Colorado real estate market.

From an architectural standpoint, our home in southern Mexico was brilliant. Our family delighted in the arched iron framed windows, the ivy–covered brick walls, the beautiful Talavera tile in the kitchen, and gorgeous stonework throughout the interior.

It was an enormous structure splendidly built for the ministry that God had called our family to accomplish in southern Mexico. It was our forever home, and we invested an abundance of personal time, effort, and finances into its renovation.

Because of Gary's death my children and I had to leave our gorgeous home and move back to Colorado where we had no home or family.

I have listed five of the most prominent secondary losses I experienced, but there are hundreds of possible losses, and every family's experience will be different. To this day, my children and I continue to identify precious things that were ripped from us as a result of Gary's death.

Identifying secondary losses helps us to process what we have lost and gain wisdom in how to move forward.

My friend Michael works in the claims department of an insurance company. He assesses the damage done by fire in residential homes. Arriving at a property, he discovers hearth and home smoldering with toxic fumes in complete ruin.

Yet, there is hope in the debris and ash. The insurance company that he works for will issue a large check guaranteeing the family's ability to buy a lovely new home. As their real estate agent, I am able to show them a beautiful home that they can purchase because of their loss.

The Lord promises to bring beauty out of ashes, but it is also important for us to assess the damage before we can fully appreciate and enjoy the coming beauty and blessing.

In fact, in the weeks and months after a tragic loss, the idea that beauty can come from our pain seems unfathomable.

I remember the day the three of us buried Gary's ashes under the lemon tree behind our home in Mexico. Nathaniel had dug a trench around the tree, and our plan was to encircle the tree with Gary's ashes.

But when I was unable to pour the ashes as planned, I was horrified to realize that bone and ash had clumped together, and I was forced to my knees in order to dig them out of the box.

His ashes covered my face while I sobbed, and his body mingled with my tears and marred my appearance as if I were a chimney sweep in Mary Poppins. But these were not ashes created from a fire on a chilly British evening; no, they were the burned body of my husband.

After my kids and I completed this horrible task, I stepped into my shower and the warm water began cascading over my head while washing Gary's ashes off my face. The mixture of ashes and tears seeped into my mouth and I will never forget the charred remains of my husband's body on my lips.

God tells us that we will experience beauty out of our ashes and joy from our grieving. He tells us that his name will be glorified, and that we will become strong oaks of righteousness.

But this will be realized in time.

It takes time to process the damage before we can walk in the cathartic beauty of the Holy Spirit's work in our lives. In the process of digging through the ashes of all of our losses, we become empowered to evaluate the devastation and eventually recognize and receive the Lord's blessings.

There is a gift of grace after loss, and I feel there are priceless treasures given to us within our sorrow if we allow ourselves to receive them.

I'm not talking about a futile search for the illusive silver lining or repeating a useless platitude by rote. I am referring to literal and remarkable occurrences that have been the direct result of bereavement.

It is important for grieving people to be able to accept the bad that has happened to them in the death of their loved one, but it is equally valuable to acknowledge the good that has come.

It seems like this would be the easy part, but it is not. It feels as though we are looking in our beloved's face and saying, "This amazing thing happened to me as a direct result of your death." It's almost as if we need everything to be horrible in order to maintain our love and devotion to the person who has died.

When the dark shadow of grief passes, we find that God turns aspects of our tragedy inside out, replacing horrific pain and evil with beauty. But is this beauty instantaneous? Does God come to the ashes of our life and in a whirlwind miracle create an immediately beautiful setting? The story of Job's life would seem to indicate otherwise: "The Lord restored Job's fortunes and gave him twice as much as he had before. . . The Lord blessed the latter part of Job's life more than the former part. He had fourteen thousand sheep, six thousand camels, a thousand yoke of oxen and a thousand donkeys. And he also had seven sons and three daughters. . . Nowhere in all the land were there found women as beautiful as Job's daughters, and their father granted them an inheritance along with their brothers. After this, Job lived a hundred and forty years; he saw his children and their children to the fourth generation. And so Job died, an old man and full of years" (Job 42:10b, 12, 15-17).

We must realize the abundance of Job's fortune and certainly his next ten children did not come to him instantly after his great losses.

We also must be cognizant of the fact, as we learned in previous chapters, our deceased loved ones can never be replaced by anyone or anything. Job and his wife enjoyed the blessing of ten babies after their other children had died, but no blessing on earth could eliminate the pain from the immensity of their previous loss.

We will always be disappointed and bitter if we are trying to make our heart stop hurting by digging through the ash box searching for gifts as a replacement.

Some aspects of my life may be sweeter than they were before Gary died, and some may be more difficult, but nothing will ever be the same. In order to receive beauty, I have learned to never compare what I have now to what I had then.

There is a common thread for those who have been delivered from the captivity and torture of war. The natural human response to being a prisoner of war is a deep yearning to be home. A nearby country will often offer a safe haven to the captive, and they will be given every comfort and resource the host nation can bestow upon them. Yet, their overwhelming desire is to eventually come home.

Seven years after my husband's death, "home" is no longer in Gary's arms. I have made peace with my bereavement and I do not expect anything to look remotely as it once did. I have a full and rewarding life as a single widowed woman.

Nevertheless, for me, the feeling of "coming home" is something I have yet to experience, as I believe it lies within the gift and sacrament of marriage.

I have been released from being a prisoner of war in the intensity of grief, and I am enjoying the delights of my host country, but I have not yet come home. I look forward to that day.

In the meantime, the Lord has given to me many beautiful gifts as he continues bringing restoration and joy into my life. Here are a few of them:

1. I've gained new friendships.

I have had a plethora of friendships that have poured into my life after Gary's death. Because my kids and I eventually moved to a new city in Colorado after Gary died, all my relationships are fresh and newly conceived during the years of intense grief.

As I ponder God's good gifts, I cannot ignore the grace of restoration, which has given me such rich and deep friendships.

2. I've gained new ministry.

My life has been abundantly blessed because of being able to open my home to others in a way that would not have been possible as a married woman. Over the past seven years, the Lord has brought precious people into my life in need of a safe haven, and I have been able play a significant role in their lives because of that. My open door has provided a refuge and a place of joy and hope.

Some of these cherished young men and women have lived with me for years, others a few months, and some have stayed for only for a weekend.

In addition, I have been blessed to be part of an altar ministry team within my church. We are a group of prayer warriors who passionately minister to those who have spiritual, emotional, or physical needs. Nothing delights my heart more than to pray God's blessing and emotional healing upon someone who is going through pain and loss. God has used me in profound ways within this outreach and I am deeply grateful for it.

The Lord has also reopened opportunities in worship ministry. When we left for Mexico I stepped out of my position as part of the worship team leadership within my church. It was difficult to have a season without an avenue for expressing my passion for praise. Therefore, it is such a blessing and a restorative joy to be part of the choir within my church in Colorado Springs.

3. I gained joy in new relationships.

When I met Gary, dating hadn't been on my radar, so I had never experienced the delight in getting to know other men in a dating environment. Gary was my first kiss and my first everything so dating after being married for eighteen years has proven to be sometimes terrifying but also a very joyful and fulfilling experience.

One relationship brought great joy and newness of life. I greatly respect this man, and when we were together, I felt I could leave the agony of death behind me. He profoundly impacted me for good. It has been an honor to know him and I cherish his presence in my life.

4. I gained a new profession.

When Gary died, I was a widowed missionary without a marketable profession. Since then I have become a successful and have enjoyed a level of affluence that I never thought possible. I have learned much through my new profession and have touched an abundance of lives.

It's hard to imagine who I would be today without the impact that my clients have had on my life—or the wide range of adventures that I have lived through in my business.

5. I gained a voice as a writer.

I have always enjoyed a deep passion for the written word. Prior to catastrophic loss my efforts in writing fell flat. Grief has given expression to my soul and has birthed words within my heart that are worthy of the page. Writing has been a profound grace and beauty given to me by the hand of God in the wake of Gary's death.

6. I gained independence.

I went directly from my parents' home into my marriage to Gary. Therefore, I never knew what it was like to be a single woman living on my own. As both of my kids are now adults, I've learned how to thrive as an independent woman. In some ways, this has been a very daunting and unwelcome change, but in other ways I have experienced a tremendous amount of freedom and fun.

I have been blessed to be able to buy the first brand–new car of my life, which is a bright blue snazzy RAV4. It climbs the most treacherous mountain roads in Colorado, and also beautifully represents my business showing luxury homes. I've always loved bright blue as a color, and it's certainly not a hue Gary would have ever chosen for a car!

I am also able to travel on a whim. I have been known to toss a few clothes into a bag and go on a spontaneous road trip to Chicago, Texas, or the Western Slope of Colorado. I am enjoying a more carefree life now that I have established my business and raised my children.

Yes, marriage will always represent truly coming home for me, but I am enjoying adventurous joy as a single woman.

What I have grown to realize is that my life after Gary's death has been a complete do-over.

I am no longer sauntering through beautiful Mexican markets hand in hand with my husband, but that doesn't mean that everything is dull and dreary and void of color and life.

My world has been transformed in painful ways I never wanted and in beautiful ways I never expected.

At first the upheaval added to my trauma and grief, but now I can perceive blessings in many of the changes.

I had a unique life as Gary's wife and as a missionary. But now I am on a completely different path. As God's grace unfolds, and I am finally able to come home, I will see that one life is not better than the other, just different.

We are not able to go through life experiencing all gains and no losses. If we never experience the journey of bereavement, then we will never experience the beauty and treasured circumstances that will occur not just despite our loss but *because of our loss*.

When untimely death befalls us, there is a flood of secondary losses which overwhelm our lives with inconceivable damage. But as the water recedes and dry ground appears, we are then able to witness the beauty of the springtime crocus blooming.

At that moment we are face to face with the glorious truth that where loss abounds the grace of God's redemption flourishes abundantly beyond what we could imagine.

Fourteen

THE PROGRESSION OF GRIEF

"Therefore, since we are surrounded by so great a cloud of witnesses... let us run with endurance and active persistence the race that is set before us, focusing our eyes on Jesus, who is the Author and Perfecter of faith."

Hebrews 12:1–3

When we walk through the untimely death of a loved one, as we have learned in previous chapters, there are many challenges that we must face. One of the more difficult challenges comes from well–meaning people who prod us to *move on* and not get *stuck* in our grief.

This was demonstrated to me recently as I sipped some tea and enjoyed a bowl of tomato soup with my friend Carol at Panera Bread. She mentioned a coworker, Beth, who she was concerned about.

Carol looked worried as she put down her baguette. "Have I told you about Beth? Her husband died of a horrible type of brain cancer in February. It was awful. And her dad died of a heart attack in April. She is extremely distraught. I see her crying in her car when she leaves work."

My eyes filled with tears as I thought of Beth and her young children. "Yeah, you had mentioned her to me," I said as I swallowed hard. "I cannot believe all that she has been through in such a short time."

"Rachel, I feel so bad for her. I think she is stuck in her grief. Can you help her?" Carol said, genuinely concerned about her friend.

I smiled as best I could, trying not to reveal the shock I felt at her words. "Carol, she's not *stuck* in her grief. In fact, it's only been a few months. Honestly, her sorrow has barely begun. She will experience overwhelming grief and sadness for many years to come."

Carol's eyes glazed over. I suspected that she was not only disregarding what I was saying now, but also that she no longer wanted me to talk to her friend.

It must have seemed overwhelming to her to think that Beth would be grieving the loss of her dad and husband for years to come. She undoubtedly didn't want to hear such a sad prognosis, and I didn't have the energy to convince her otherwise.

As I often did in situations like this, I turned back to my hot tea and tomato soup and changed the subject. As she chatted about her children, I wondered what Carol would have thought about the tears of grief that I had shed that very morning, which I still do on occasion nearly eight years after Gary's death.

Those of us who have lost deeply often face the prodding of friends and family who cannot walk the distance of the journey with us. As grieving people, we feel bewilderment and shame, as though something is wrong with us because we are not able to *move on* a few months or even *a few years* after our spouse's death.

The truth is that Beth will never *move on,* but she will move forward. Beth's husband will continue to be a part of her life as she moves forward through her grief.

Because of the life Gary and I shared and the children we raised together, he will always be present with me. I see him in our children and how much they resemble him in spirit and personality. He is present in my home even though he never shared this particular house with me. He is present with me in worship, prayer, and most certainly in Bible study. He is present in our family life, in the traditions that we carry on and in the things that we value and the jokes that my children and I share.

The threads of Gary's life and death will remain inexorably part of the tapestry of my story in treasured and precious ways.

When a loved one dies (even when we have the horrendous experience of digging their ashes out of a box and burying them under a lemon tree), we do not feel as though they have ceased to exist. We often have an awareness of their soul being irrefutably real in heaven. This is not only hope based on Scripture—we actually sense their presence with us.

It might even feel as though our loved ones have been deployed to heaven, as someone in the military may be deployed to Iraq or Afghanistan.

We have made our family home in Colorado Springs which has a strong military presence. We have the coveted Air Force Academy, Peterson Air Force Base, Schriever Air Force Base, Fort Carson Army Base, and of course NORAD, responsible for delighting children since 1955 by "tracking" the travels of Santa and his reindeer every year on December 24!

The military impacts every aspect of life in Colorado Springs from our churches to our real estate market.

Because of this, many of my friends and clients have a military background. When they talk about the pain of being separated from a deployed spouse, their feelings resonate with me. Oddly, I can relate to much of what they feel.

While deployed spouses can sometimes be reached for a video chat, those who have been bereaved are not so delusional as to think that we can have an online meeting with our loved ones in heaven. At the same time, our loved one has not ceased to exist.

Gary is still very present with me and my children. Death for the believer is not the end but rather a new beginning in heaven.

I would like to share a personal story that impacted my dear friend Andrea and me on a crisp Saturday morning in October. Andrea's brother Armand had died at the young age of thirty-four just two years prior to Gary's death.

This particular Saturday, Andrea and I were attending a teaching session in the Watchman Training Center at the missions organization Every Home for Christ.

Andrea suddenly looked at me during the worship time and whispered, "Did you feel that?"

I *had* felt something! I couldn't put words to it, but I had absolutely felt in the spirit that something precious had just occurred.

"Yes, I did!" I responded.

In a hushed whisper she began to describe what she had just experienced. "As we were singing, I could almost see Armand and Gary looking down on us. I knew that they were together in heaven, and I could sense how excited and overjoyed they are about our friendship."

Her words resonated with me. I nodded in agreement as sobs wracked my body.

That moment when her brother and my husband were looking down upon us from heaven will always stand out in our friendship. There was no doubt in either one of our minds that Armand and Gary are real and tangible men who love us deeply but whose residence is now in heaven.

Gary's and Armond's deployment to heaven did not remove their love for us nor ours for them.

John wrote, "In my Father's house are many rooms. If it were not so, would I have told you that I go to prepare a place for you?" (John 14:2 ESV).

Paul reiterates this idea when he writes, "But our citizenship is in heaven, and from it we await a savior, the Lord Jesus Christ, who will transform our lowly body to be like his glorious body" (Philippians 3:20 ESV) and "For me to live is Christ and to die is gain. If I am to live in the flesh, that means fruitful labor for me. Yet, which shall I choose I cannot tell. I am hard pressed between the two. My desire is to depart and be with Christ for that is far better" (Philippians 1:21).

These verses and many more like them give tremendous hope and joy to the believer. These verses reveal to us that our spouse, brother, sibling, or parent is alive in heaven at this very moment. They have not ceased to exist. They have been deployed to a spiritual realm.

Therefore, after we bury the ashes of our husband or wife, we cannot and *should not* attempt to *move on* as if we had just flushed a goldfish down the toilet.

But we will *always* be moving forward.

Telling anyone who has buried a loved one that they need to *move on* is not helpful. And, for the widow or widower, because of the unique union that marriage creates, it is also impossible, as the following aptly illustrates: "For this reason a man shall leave his father and his mother, and be joined to his wife; and they shall become one flesh" (Genesis 2:24 NASB).

When a spouse dies, we are torn apart. Many husbands and wives who have stood next to the pool of blood at the scene of an accident or lain beside a loved one on the hospice bed describe the pain that they feel as *gut-wrenching*. No matter how strong the vocabulary, no words can adequately describe the demolishing effects of the death of a spouse upon our lives.

When Gary and I were in ministry together, I often tried to empathize with grieving widows and widowers who came to us for counsel. However, after Gary's death I realized that my understanding and empathy had fallen short.

Let me share two metaphors, one I had believed to be clever and accurate prior to Gary's death, and the second I have come to understand through my own personal loss.

One of my passions and talents is cooking. I can enter a kitchen full of chaotic ingredients and a couple hours later present a gourmet meal. It is always a creative delight for me to cook something delicious, which is why I often think in terms of the kitchen when trying to understand the complexities of life.

Before Gary died, when I struggled to comprehend what the widows and widowers around me were experiencing, I came up with an analogy that I thought would help me to understand their journey. In my imagination this involved taking apart a pan of my homemade lasagna.

I pictured Gary walking into our kitchen, his eyes clamped on a pan of delicious bubbling homemade lasagna, as the two of us would begin to separate it.

First, Gary would grab a few Pyrex mixing bowls out of the cupboard and he would scoop off the parmesan cheese and put it into a bowl, and next would come the meat sauce that he would scoop into a separate bowl. We would continue this process into the early evening.

The operation of taking apart a hot pan of bubbling lasagna would make an enormous mess in my kitchen and I, being the more clumsy one, would undoubtedly get burned in the process. But because Gary and I worked well together this project would also be pleasant and fun.

After all the bowls had been filled and the kitchen put back into order, we would have a container of various cheeses, a container of meat sauce, and a container of noodles. Later in the evening, I can just picture Gary sneaking into our kitchen and gobbling up some of my delicious lasagna even if it had been torn apart and dumped into bowls.

However, since Gary's death, I have found this endearing imaginative story lacking. I have since learned that it is impossible to separate the union of two people because the bonds of marriage have blended them into one person.

In my fanciful story, the separated lasagna ingredients could have been used for other purposes if we so desired. Gary and I could have made delicious spaghetti with the Italian sausage meat sauce, chicken Alfredo with the cheeses, and a variation of macaroni and cheese with the pasta.

Yes, they would all resemble their previous marriage to the lasagna, but the lasagna ingredients could *move on* into other delicious recipes and no one would ever know that they had at one time been part of a pan of lasagna.

This is all fine and dandy except for the fact that the union of marriage makes the separation of ingredients impossible. I have found marriage to resemble a chocolate fudge cake more closely than it does a pan of lasagna.

In marriage our bodies and our lives become one entity. In this metaphor, Gary's and my marriage would have consisted of eggs, flour, sugar, cocoa, vanilla, butter, and leavening. When I used to make a chocolate fudge cake for Gary's birthday, I could not wake up the following morning and extract the eggs to make breakfast for my kiddos. In the same way, it would not be possible to remove the sugar to put in my coffee.

Becoming one person is the essence of marriage. For eighteen years, the unity in my marriage created a delicious chocolate fudge cake. I can no more pull that cake apart and salvage the ingredients than I am able to salvage a specific part of Gary's body from his ashes.

Because of the unity of marriage, I am no longer a separate person with individual ingredients, but I will always be part of the cake of the union of *Gary and Rachel*. I will always contain aspects of the eggs, flour, sugar, cocoa, vanilla, butter, and leavening from Gary's and my marriage.

When people tell a widow or widower to *move on*, I think of the illustration of the lasagna. They are asking their grieving friend or family member to pull their deceased spouse from their life and *move on*, leaving the previous marriage behind.

However, like a delicious chocolate fudge cake, we cannot be torn apart from our deceased spouse.

Since marriage is less like lasagna and more like chocolate cake, what does this mean for future relationships?

What this means is that, while grief will always be with us to one degree or another, as we move forward our memories will become less debilitating. And as we continue to give time and expression to grief, we may experience the natural flow of life and love and move forward into another marriage if we desire to do so.

I do not believe there is a magic number of years when it is suddenly the correct time to be in another relationship. That will vary from person to person, and also depend on the intimate details surrounding their loss.

But when we stop thinking of *moving on*—and start thinking about moving forward, we will be better able to give ourselves unreservedly to another person in time.

I love what Anne Lamott writes in *Operating Instructions: A Journal of My Son's First Year*: "And I felt like my heart had been so thoroughly and irreparably broken that there could be no real joy again, that at best there might eventually be a little contentment. Everyone wanted me to get help and rejoin life, pick up the pieces and move on, and I tried to, I wanted to, but I just had to lie in the mud with my arms wrapped around myself, eyes closed, grieving, until I didn't have to anymore."

It was five years after Gary's death before I allowed myself the delights of falling in love again. I didn't learn to *move on* by falling in love. Instead, moving forward into another relationship was the natural outflow of the time and expression that I had given to grief.

What I've observed is that, when widows and widowers begin to date, early conversation include the stories of how their spouses died. Even in a casual "getting to know each other" scenario where there would more typically be flirtatious banter, the conversation becomes hushed, beautiful, and sacred.

And when widows and widowers marry, they often share a deep sense of reverence and honor regarding the previous husband and wife who have died. The deceased spouse can be beloved and cherished even in the new marriage, with special memories kept alive and perhaps even photos displayed.

It is not healthy to build a shrine to the previous marriage, but neither is it healthy *or possible* to pretend that the deceased spouse did not exist.

Which brings me to the experience of divorce. I have intentionally entrusted the painful subject of divorce to other authors. Because death and divorce are such different experiences, I felt that any attempt to *combi*ne the two types of losses in one book would fall short.

But let me comment on one thing.

While divorce rips people apart, it is typically caused by wounds inflicted by the couple upon each other. As a result, it is unlikely that a divorced person finds themselves honoring and cherishing their former spouse.

However, when death rips people apart, it is often disease or an accident that has taken a beloved partner away. As a result, in bereavement the previous husband or wife is often cherished and revered.

This is an important distinction. Because of our divorce–saturated society, divorce is much more common than the untimely death of a spouse.

I believe this is why well–meaning onlookers advise the bereaved in the same way they advise someone who is divorced. But as you can imagine, *moving on* after divorce looks vastly different from moving forward after bereavement. It is imperative that we make this distinction. Otherwise, friends and family will expect the journey of bereavement to mirror that of divorce.

I mentioned earlier that while it's impossible to pretend a deceased spouse never existed, it's also not healthy to have our homes frozen in the past is if they were a museum.

How do we know when it is endearing to treasure a reminder of the person lost and when it is unhealthy?

Is there a rule book that we can order on Amazon that will tell us what photos to hang on a wall and what to store away in a drawer?

How do we know what will damage a future marriage?

What previous memories can coexist with the new?

A few years ago, when I arrived home after spending a beautiful evening with the man I was dating, I put Gary's PJs on and climbed into my bed. This made me feel close to Gary, but it was a binding closeness and not a healthy one.

Wearing his clothes kept me in bondage to the past. After many months, I gathered up Gary's PJs, his glasses, and a few other personal items, put them in a bag and laid them quietly in our trash can. I struggled to do this, but it was an important step in my ability to move forward.

There are various items of clothing, family dishes, and our home library that have Gary's fingerprints all over them. Does this mean that I need to get rid of all these things before entering another relationship? Absolutely not.

But I take the heart connections associated with these items seriously. I have already given many of these things to Nathaniel and Bethany who are able to cherish them without Gary's treasured belongings hindering their future lives as they would mine.

Figuring these things out can be difficult. Many of us desire a list of dos and don'ts. The only guideline for moving forward is to be ever mindful of our actions and whether they progress us forward or hold us back. There is no statute of "right and wrong" where grief is concerned.

Therefore, when we read a book, attend a class, or talk with a church counselor, we need to carefully assess who is giving us advice and whether they know what they are talking about.

Many well–intentioned people believe they understand how to grieve well as they prod us to *move on*, but the grief of bereavement is something that only those who have walked through it can understand. We need to be wary of advice given by those who have never even cracked the lid off the sewer of bereavement and taken a whiff of the agony of our grief.

The human drive to move forward is astonishing. There is a deep courage and tenacity of the living to move forward after the death of a loved one. Therefore, I do not believe that we need to worry so much about getting *stuck* in grief. The last thing that grieving people desire is to stay in the depths of the pain in which they find themselves.

What most people perceive as being *stuck* in grief is very often the normal progression and timeline that loss follows.

Grief is much lengthier than anyone would like to believe and so the automatic response to assume that a bereaved friend or relative is somehow not *moving on* as they should.

We must give the grieving process adequate time and expression for our wounded hearts to heal. When we do the work of time and expression required by grief, we will be propelled forward into newness of life.

When I think of moving forward, I think of wise words uttered by Bilbo in *The Hobbit*:

"'Go back?' he thought. 'No good at all! Go sideways? Impossible! Go forward? Only thing to do! On we go!' So up he got and trotted along with his little sword held in front of him and one hand feeling the wall, and his heart all of a patter and a pitter.'"

Fifteen

THE PROMISE OF GRIEF

*"He will wipe away every tear from their eyes, and death
shall be no more, neither shall there be mourning, nor crying,
nor pain anymore, for the former things have passed away."*

Revelation 21:4

From my office I watch the snow gently falling outside of my
Colorado home. Flames in the fireplace warm my office. I am
a sucker for the texture and sound a wood–burning fire creates
(despite the bits of unwanted bark and ash).

My fingers wrap around my red mug and I savor the aroma of my
favorite dark roast coffee. I see the pages of my manuscript lying upon
a bright red side table, a tangible tribute to the intensity of effort in
putting pen to paper—or fingers to keyboard as it may be.

On this beautiful December morning, I am overflowing with joy to
be living the life that God has given to me.

I am not thinking these things because I am momentarily caught
up in the warm glow of seasonal festivities.

I really *have* been delightfully blessed in these seven years since
Gary's death, and I feel grateful for this in every season, not just during
the holidays.

However, despite the beauty and the blessings, there is a subtle and relentless ache in my heart. I feel an unrest that I cannot explain. Often there is sadness and occasionally depression that I battle in my life.

But why is this? What is the source of the barrenness I experience?

Henry David Thoreau writes in *Life in the Woods*: "The mass of men lead lives of quiet desperation."

While I don't agree with everything Thoreau has written, I completely concede to his observation that there is a hidden anguish that casts a shadow over our lives.

Many of our experiences are tainted and the longings of our heart are often in conflict with painful realities around us. Sometimes we can pinpoint the source of our anguish—such as when we receive a tragic diagnosis of cancer—and sometimes we feel the presence of pain and loss even when we don't know why. Either way, there never seems to be a day or experience that is truly free from concern or pain.

The feeling of being haunted by unrest is not reserved only for those who experience catastrophic loss. We can also experience small daily frustrations that nibble away at our peace.

In fact, before Gary died, he and I often walked through these kinds of nagging situations that hijacked the joy within our marriage.

Days that might have been peaceful and pleasant are interrupted by a flat tire, a broken dishwasher, an argument with a friend, or the cat puking on the carpet. It's as if an annoying dog is biting at our ankles. He is too small to be dangerous but strong enough to ruin and frustrate what should be a peaceful walk in a lovely park.

At some point in our human experience, our hearts cry out, *But it's not supposed to be this way!* There is a deep sense of justice within us that believes tragedies such as death, disease, and divorce are not supposed to invade our lives.

When we watch the classic animated Disney movies, the captivating ending line is *And they lived happily ever after.* The writers and producers get it right, because these stories resonate with how deep in our hearts we feel life is supposed to be. We want to meet our prince, or rescue our princess, and then life will be joyful and absent of struggle. We are always hoping to *live happily ever after.*

But when we wake up on Monday morning, the hope of a fairytale life quickly fades. We cannot escape the fact that our stories—and the stories of those around us—are burdened with trials and struggles.

In the very depths of our souls, we have a God–instilled belief that life should be overflowing with true love, honor, happiness, and peace.

But our human experience shows us that this not the case.

Surprisingly, even traditional wedding vows bring a dose of harsh reality into the joy–filled promises that we proclaim to our beloved as we say phrases like these: *In sickness and health* or *for richer or poorer.* Mentioning illness and poverty in a wedding vow certainly doesn't conjure up visions of happily ever after.

Yet we promise to be faithful because somehow, we know that *life is pain* and can include many hardships. Our marriage vows are not only to love and honor the person who makes our hearts go pitter patter, they also bind us to a commitment of faithfulness as we walk through the trials and tribulations of life.

While we're on the subject of wedding vows, let's take an imaginative look at the first "wedding" ever, that of Adam and Eve. Of course, they didn't exchange vows as we know them but, if they had, those vows wouldn't have had to include phrases like *in sickness and in health, for better or worse,* or *for richer or poorer.*

Why? Because they lived in a perfect world.

At least until things went awry.

But before we talk about that, let's look closer at the world of beauty and perfection that God created for the very first couple. "Then the LORD God planted a garden in Eden, in the east, and there he placed the man he had made. The LORD God made all sorts of trees grow up from the ground—trees that were beautiful and that produced delicious fruit" (Genesis 2:8–9 NLT).

As we ponder Eden, we can assume that we were not created for a life of affliction, struggle, and difficulty. Instead we were created to thrive and love and create in an unspoiled and stunning environment.

There's something else I want to point out about that verse. Let's revisit the first sentence:

"The LORD God planted a garden. . ."

God *planted*!

It is challenging to wrap our minds around what we have just read. The power of the spoken Word of God birthed the universe, but when it came to vegetables, God dug up soil and stuck seeds in the ground!

Can you imagine what flowers cultivated by the creator of billions of galaxies looked like? Are we able to picture God planting row after row of carrots? And what array of flowers must have blossomed from the touch of his hands!

Gary and I were avid gardeners. We planted and cared for twenty-seven unique and beautiful rose bushes. We tended a sizable vegetable garden as well as many flowerbeds throughout our land which we affectionately called Mooreview Park. This beautiful foliage was planted by human hands in the difficult Colorado clay soil.

My imagination goes wild in thinking of a garden cultivated by the hands of God.

We were conceived for a perfect world full of beauty, fellowship with God, and peaceful interaction with men and animals.

After God breathed life into Adam, he immediately gave him a creative task: name all the animals! In the process, Adam embraced the adventure of finding a creative solution to a more personal need, which was to find a mate. "The man gave names to all the livestock, the birds of the sky and all the wild animals. But for Adam no suitable helper was found (Genesis 2:20).

I love that God infused within us a desire for adventure, intimacy, sexual expression, problem-solving, and creativity.

And by creating us in his own image, God also gave us the capacity for inventive thinking, artistic design, music, and the satisfaction of working with others toward a common goal.

Not only was Eden perfect but God gave it to Adam and Eve as a fertile environment in which they could use their many gifts to invent, cultivate, and create.

The implications of what God intended for mankind are mind-boggling.

We were designed for Eden—not urban decay, disease, violence, and crime.

The world we were created to enjoy no longer exists and therefore there is an unmet longing in our souls.

We have creation in our hearts, and everything within our being aches for our world to be as it once was but is no longer.

Unfortunately, as you and I know all too well, our world is broken, and life is painfully difficult.

So what happened?

What happened is that Adam and Eve brought corruption into that world.

When Adam and Eve rebelled against God they brought the tragic effects of sin crashing down upon their lives, as well as the lives of their children, their children's children, and beyond. Adam and Eve's rebellion not only severed their relationship with God but also brought destruction and eventual death to every life since that time.

Sin mangled the beauty of God's creation and our ability to find fulfillment in it.

In *our* world, jobs are lost, cancer is diagnosed, and divorce happens.

We are fractured. We are broken.

Sin has a corrosive effect that destroys the beauty and virtue God intended for us.

I am reminded of the Russian Revolution and a storyline in the *Downton Abbey* series. Prince Kuragin, once part of the noble elite, finds himself with other Russian refugees stripped of power and prestige, attempting to ease their poverty and desperation.

At one point of despair, Prince Kuragin explains to the Countess of Grantham, "When you go through a storm like ours, you give up hope quite early in the proceedings."

"I agree," she says knowingly. "Hope is a tease, designed to prevent us accepting reality."

We, like Prince Kuragin, are born for greatness and beauty but find ourselves trapped within a life of silent desperation.

We have a passionate hunger in our heart for things to be made right and for life to function as it is supposed to.

We yearn for Eden and we are left feeling the nagging pain of what life should be—but is not.

We have a bucket list of wonderful things we would like to experience before we die. We desire to wander down the cobblestone streets of Italy or go ice fishing on a gorgeous mountain lake in Alaska. We believe these unique, unfamiliar experiences may give us a few moments or hours when we can experience peace and relish a glimpse into life as it was meant to be.

But even the most wonderful moments in life are often mingled with disappointment.

The experience itself can fail to meet our expectations. And even if it exceeds our wildest dreams, at the end of the vacation we discover that pain remains our companion, or grief is waiting for us as we step off the plane, and our problems haven't gone away at all. And we are quickly jolted out of these unspoiled moments back into our fallen and sin–filled existence.

We will be perpetually crushed by the weight of disappointment if we continue trying to fill the emptiness by grasping at circumstances, experiences, or things.

If wonderful moments, spouses, or children can't fill the aching hole in our lives what or who can?

I have heard it said that we are born with a God–shaped hole in our heart and the only thing that will fill that space is Jesus. I agree that faith in Jesus is the only means for the weight of sin to be removed from our lives, and that his presence with us brings a hope and peace that is beyond comprehension.

But as believers we may silently resign ourselves to the reality that not even God removes all of the desperate longing with which we live.

When we are talking about the prevailing pain and longing that is present in our lives, there is an additional component we must consider. And there is something more to the story of our redemption that we often miss.

C.S. Lewis gives us a beautiful explanation of this in his book, *Mere Christianity*, when he talks about the kinds of things we desire. He says that we are not born with random desires for which no satisfaction may be found. He says, for example, that babies crave food, ducks long to swim, and men and women feel sexual desire because the fulfillment of these needs/desires is possible. The thing that is longed for actually exists.

He goes on to say that if we experience a longing that cannot be met within the confines of this world, it's probably because our world was never *meant* to satisfy that longing; indeed, it's likely because we were made for another world.

Of these longings, he writes: "Probably earthly pleasures were never meant to satisfy it, but only to arouse it, to suggest the real thing."

Lewis adds, "I must keep alive in myself the desire for my true country, which I shall not find till after death; I must never let it get snowed under or turned aside; I must make it the main object of life to press on to that country and to help others to do the same."

The fact is Eden is lost. But there is a future paradise that we have been promised in which we will once again experience unfettered fellowship with God in a perfect and pain–free world.

In fact, Jesus talks about our eternal home when he says, "And if I go and prepare a place for you, I will come back and take you to be with me that you also may be where I am" (John 14:3).

This is the true country to which Lewis refers, the other world for which we long. In fact, the longing for eternity has been passionately engraved upon our hearts by the finger of God.

Throughout Scripture we are encouraged to view our circumstances through the filter of knowing that something amazing awaits us. In fact, Paul contrasts his suffering with the weight of heavenly glory that was being stored up for him: "For our light and momentary troubles are achieving for us an eternal glory that far outweighs them all. So we fix our eyes not on what is seen, but on what is unseen, since what is seen is temporary, but what is unseen is eternal" (2 Corinthians 4:17–18).

Paul is revealing to us the value of looking to eternity—and not to our surroundings—for contentment and joy.

As we anticipate the pristine perfection of heaven, we are empowered to feel joy and contentment despite our current troubles.

Conversely, if we look to the world around us for joy and contentment, we will be burdened with misery and disappointment.

This is not a difficult concept to grasp intellectually. The challenge lies as we grapple with it in day–to–day life.

The moment our hearts accept the fact that *happily ever after* will take place in eternity, we will stop expecting to find it in Colorado, Texas, or New York—or even Alaska or Italy!

Seeing our world through an eternal perspective is like receiving sight after blindness. We are able to experience peace and hope despite our adversities.

Because of this, we are able to embrace both the blessings and trials of this world with joyful abandon:

- We can dance until the last song is played . . . even if we had a flat tire on the way to the wedding.
- We can twirl with delight while wearing a pretty dress. . . even if the cat puked earlier that day.
- We can sing in the rain. . . even if we have a nagging cough.
- We can be enraptured by sexual intimacy with our spouses . . . even if we argued that morning.
- We can be deliriously happy. . . even though, while God created us for perfection, we live in a fallen world.

Even when we have a relationship with Jesus, the difficulties of life do not disappear and the longing in our hearts for the world as it was created to be does not change. But he will walk alongside us and bring us a peace that we cannot comprehend as we look toward eternity and life as it was meant to be.

Here's what the Bible says we get to look forward to:

I saw the Holy City, the new Jerusalem, coming down out of heaven from God, prepared as a bride beautifully dressed for her husband. And I heard a loud voice from the throne saying, "Look! God's dwelling place is now among the people, and he will dwell with them. They will be his people, and God himself will be with them and be their God. 'He will wipe every tear from their eyes. There will be no more death' or mourning or crying or pain, for the old order of things has passed away." (Revelation 21:2–4)

The wolf will live with the lamb. The leopard will lie down with the goat. The calf and the lion and the yearling together. The cow will feed with the bear, their young will lie down together, and the lion will eat straw like the ox. The infant will play near the cobra's den and the young child will put its hand into the viper's nest. They will neither harm nor destroy on all my holy mountain, for the earth will be filled with the knowledge of the LORD as the waters cover the sea. (Isaiah 11:6–9)

He will wipe away every tear from their eyes, and death shall be no more, neither shall there be mourning, nor crying, nor pain anymore, for the former things have passed away. (Revelation 21:4 ESV)

At the end of all things, our unmet longings will be fulfilled. The hidden anguish will be no more. The subtle and relentless ache will disappear.

We will no longer be haunted by unrest but will be completely fulfilled as we spend eternity in paradise with God in the glory of his new creation. The completion of God's purpose through Jesus will result in the restoration of humans to their place as co-rulers of the world, ready to enjoy the beauty and peace of Eden. We will take the new creation into uncharted territory unmarred by sin, death, and pain.

And we will echo C.S. Lewis's triumphant words written in *The Last Battle*:

"I have come home at last! This is my real country! I belong here. This is the land I have been looking for all my life, though I never knew it till now. . . Come further up, come further in!"

Sixteen

A WAY IN THE WILDERNESS

"Do not call to mind the former things, or ponder things of the past. Behold, I will do something new, Now it will spring forth; Will you not be aware of it? I will even make a pathway in the wilderness, Rivers in the desert."

Isaiah 43:18–19 NASB

Once a year when we were young children, my sister Naomi and I impatiently endured the two-hour drive to the Allegheny National Forest in Pennsylvania with our parents.

All year long we looked forward to this camping trip. When we would arrive in the majestic forest, my sister and I would wrestle with setting up the big army tent. Once camp was established, we would race to climb the large moss-covered glacier rocks, and explore mysterious wooded paths shrouded by a low-hanging canopy of dense trees.

For some reason, our parents insisted we couldn't go swimming until the day had heated up to the magical temperature of seventy-two degrees. I have to confess that my sister and I were not above trying to heat up the thermometer with our hands, coaxing it to show a higher temperature than the cool mountain air would suggest.

Our joy was almost tangible as Naomi and I would walk the long creaky wooden bridge to the beautiful swimming lake. The snowmelt cascaded down from the Appalachian Mountains and was shockingly frigid, but it only made us more excited to brave the cold water together. The beauty was astounding, and our adventures never ending.

The wilderness areas of the Pennsylvania mountains are deep, rich, and beautiful.

Gary and I lived in the beautiful town of Estes Park, Colorado, and had annual passes to Rocky Mountain National Park. On many weekends we tossed our young children into our blue Subaru and headed into the mountains.

When we located a hiking area Gary would take the lead while I followed, and our children walked protected between us.

On occasion, we could feel the haunting presence of a mountain lion nearby. In these situations, Gary and I would give each other a knowing look as I would begin to lead Nathaniel and Bethany in a rollicking song which typically concluded with much laughter from our kiddos.

Nathaniel and Bethany never knew that their mother's love of singing while hiking was partially due to a healthy fear of the Colorado wildlife. These remote hikes took us past ponderosa pines, the quaking aspens, and a plethora of wildflowers. We crossed rivers, viewed unusual birds, and witnessed the immense beauty of the Rocky Mountains.

Undoubtedly, our hikes also took us past bears and mountain lions who warily avoided a tasty human snack because of this crazy lady's singing.

The Colorado wilderness is rugged, beautiful, and awe inspiring.

During our life as missionaries in the remote areas of southern Mexico, our courageous family sought out areas to explore.

Not far from our home, we found a steep mountain trail that led to a true tropical paradise. And since hiking was not the cultural norm where we lived, this unspoiled location became our family's secret hideaway.

The path wound steeply down to an isolated river full of lush plants, flowers and, yes, tropical insects. But other than being repulsed by a few enormous arachnids, we found ourselves amazed at the beauty of the orange, yellow, and bright green insects that none of us had ever seen before.

Gary and I carefully traversed the rocks that led us through the river. But Nathaniel and Bethany, being thrilled with the adventurous life that they were leading as missionary kids, bounded into the clear mountain water. With delightful abandon they enjoyed the remote tropical wilderness.

We climbed through immense foliage and discovered full grown trees that I'd only seen as houseplants in Colorado. The allure of the tropical Mexican wilderness was incredible and unlike anything we had ever experienced.

The Mexican wilderness is lush, vibrant, and stunning.

When I sit on my deck and open the pages of my Bible and read about any wilderness, my heart naturally travels to the above-mentioned beloved destinations, and I feel the peace and joy that my memories evoke.

Yet, this is not what God is talking about in Isaiah when he refers to "wilderness." Here's what He says: "Do not call to mind the former things, or ponder things of the past. Behold, I will do something new, now it will spring forth; will you not be aware of it? I will even make a roadway in the wilderness, rivers in the desert" (Isaiah 43:18–19 NASB).

Isaiah was written in the desert area of the Middle East. The Hebrew word used for *wilderness* and *desert* is *midbar*. It is used over 300 times in Scripture. The definition for *midbar* is "complete utter desolation, a wasteland, or to be totally stripped."

> Some wandered in desert wastelands [midbar], finding no way to a city where they could settle. They were hungry and thirsty, and their lives ebbed away. Then they cried out to the LORD in their trouble. (Psalm 107:4–6)

> The desert [midbar] and the parched land will be glad; the wilderness [midbar] will rejoice and blossom. . . Water will gush forth in the wilderness [midbar] and streams in the desert. The burning sand will become a pool, the thirsty ground bubbling springs. (Isaiah 35:1, 6–7)

The Hebrew word *midbar* describes for us a situation of bleak barrenness where life is void of vegetation, flowers, trees, and water.

When we have experienced tragic loss, we find ourselves in a wilderness of complete ruin. Our lips are parched and there is darkness all around. There is an abyss of devastation and sorrow that consumes us.

God's beloved people find themselves facing their own tremendous loss in these kinds of circumstances as God speaks to them through the pages of Isaiah.

I'd like to point out that God's promise of a river flowing through a barren wasteland is remarkable. What Isaiah is describing would have been bewildering to the Middle Eastern reader familiar with the surrounding barren deserts. After all, even if there is a torrential rain in the desert, the water will run off the parched ground at a rapid pace and any hint of moisture will evaporate in the scorching heat.

Therefore, what Isaiah is describing probably seemed absurd to the reader of his time. Isaiah is stating that suddenly beyond our wildest imaginations, God will bring into a wasteland a tropical paradise bursting with gorgeous sunsets, abundant vegetation, and a sparkling river winding through the suddenly lush terrain as far as the eye can see.

The only way this could be possible is through the miraculous. It is God himself who will do this great work of beauty and provision. For the Israelites this abundant river would make worthless land usable, and it would mean their current location was flourishing and they wouldn't need to move (possibly to lands that were not their own) for water.

Because of God's promise we are encouraged to stop focusing our attention on the suffering of the past but to look to him and watch him do a stunning new thing.

This portion of Scripture is written with such anticipation that we can nearly hear the author's excitement in writing what the Holy Spirit is showing him. As Isaiah writes these words, I can imagine his eyes wide with belief in the God who is showing him the promise of new life:

"Do you not perceive it? Will you not give heed to it?"

A few weeks after my husband's horrific death in Southern Mexico, I awakened early. My dazed and sleepy mind gradually grasped the sweet melody of the tropical birds and the pungent fragrance of guava trees.

I stumbled to our kitchen and, a few minutes later, over a cup of coffee I began to quietly pour my heart out to the Lord in prayer.

"Oh God, what am I to do? How am I to survive without my husband? It's not fair! It wasn't supposed to be this way! We are on the mission field. My life feels totally barren and desolate."

I stared through a wall of windows into the surrounding jungle as the sun rose over the mountains and began to bring definition to the tropical foliage. In those moments, God spoke the promises from Isaiah clearly to my heart. His voice was loving and restorative in nature. "I am about to do something new. See, I have already begun! Do you not see it? I will make a pathway through the wilderness. I will create rivers in the dry wasteland" (Isaiah 43:19 NLT).

Since Gary had died, there had not been one moment in which I had not felt gut-wrenching pain and the complete annihilation of life as I had known it. I was stunned to hear God's words of hope only weeks after my husband's death.

At that time, my life was a wilderness in every sense of the word. I desperately needed the Lord's rivers of life flowing through the desolation that death had created.

I left my coffee and got up from my place of prayer. I walked to one of the windowpanes that my husband had replaced during our renovation project. Where he had grasped the pane of glass, I could still see the faint outline of his fingerprints. I softly placed my fingers on the glass where his had been and wept.

I trusted in God's cathartic words even when I couldn't feel his presence or envision any hope for my future.

A river watering the garden flowed from Eden; from there it was separated into four headwaters. The name of the first is the Pishon; it winds through the entire land of Havilah, where there is gold. (The gold of that land is good; aromatic resin and onyx are also there.) The name of the second river is the Gihon; it winds through the entire land of Cush. The name of the third river is the Tigris; it runs along the east side of Ashur. And the fourth river is the Euphrates. (Genesis 2:10–14)

God paints a beautiful picture of these rivers that brought life to the garden of Eden. It is this type of river full of his promises that he causes to flow into the devastation of our lives. These are waterways full of hope and overflowing with reclamation.

The picture that we see from Genesis to Revelation is full of restoration and grace. These rivers in the desolate wilderness that Isaiah speaks of are full of God's promises to his people that he will bring rivers of living water into the desolation of their lives. These rivers will provide rest, beauty, and joy. The rivers in the desert are not negligible streams trickling a tiny ration of provision. They are wild beautiful raging rivers full of God's love, grace, and resurrection life.

We find another astonishing picture of restoration in Job: "For there is hope for a tree, when it is cut down, that it will sprout again, and its shoots will not fail. Though its roots grow old in the ground and its stump dies in the dry soil, at the scent of water it will flourish again and put forth sprigs like a young plant" (Job 14:7 NASB).

Recently I spent a week planting hundreds of saplings at a friend's mountain cabin. Her family's land had been destroyed in one of Colorado's many forest fires. As we planted the young trees, we were surrounded by dead and burned stumps. There is no possible way, outside of the miraculous, that one of these dead burned stumps could have sprouted with new life.

What God is promising Job is completely unexpected and out of the order of nature. There is a profound feeling of anticipation and restorative power in these verses tucked into passages describing Job's horrific experience of death and disease.

At the mere *scent* of water, new life will spring forth and make a dead tree stump alive again!

In a similar way, water is a surprise in a desert. It's something you don't expect to find, so when God provides it, it's spectacular and miraculous!

But something you *do* expect to find in a barren wasteland is rocks. Lots of rocks! And yet even this thing that is so common as we journey through the wilderness of grief God uses to reveal spectacular, miraculous truths about himself!

In my journey through the wilderness, here is what rocks have symbolized to me:

- Hope and help
- Remembrance and thankfulness
- Loss, surrender, and death
- Finally, resurrection life

Let's take a look at each of these.

We see in Psalms that David understood that God was his only strength, his only hope, and his only refuge—and he described that strength and hope as a rock and fortress:

"The Lord is my rock and my fortress and my deliverer; my God, my rock, in whom I take refuge; my shield, and the horn of my salvation, my stronghold" (Psalm 18:2).

"For who is God, but the Lord? And who is a rock, except our God?" (Psalm 18:31 ESV).

He is "my rock, and exalted be the God of my salvation" (Psalm 18:46 ESV). In this case, a rock is a symbol of strength and permanency.

Then, in Joshua 4, we see rocks used to represent remembrance and thanksgiving. While taking them (finally!) into the promised land, God beckons the Israelites to cross the Jordan River which, at that time of year, would have been in flood stage. Miraculously God provided a passage of dry ground through the dangerous river. Joshua then requests that each of the twelve family groups remove large stones from the Jordan riverbed and carry them to the promised land where the rocks would be stacked in a pile:

"Take up twelve stones from the middle of the Jordan, from right where the priests are standing, and carry them over with you and put them down at the place where you stay tonight. . . . In the future, when your children ask you, 'What do these stones mean?' tell them that the flow of the Jordan was cut off before the ark of the covenant of the LORD. When it crossed the Jordan, the waters of the Jordan were cut off. These stones are to be a memorial to the people of Israel forever." (Joshua 4:3, 6–7)

These rocks were a memorial to God's love and miraculous provision.

We see stones being used another time to commemorate God's love and provision in Samuel 7, after God gave the Israelites victory over the Philistines. "Then Samuel took a stone and set it up between Mizpah and Shen. He named it Ebenezer, saying, 'Thus far the LORD has helped us'" (1 Samuel 7:12).

Samuel recognized the source of their victory and publicly declared it. By commemorating God's goodness in a permanent way, it ensured that the Israelites would be reminded of God's grace and love for them.

In the examples above, the rocks described are symbolic of God's redemption, affection, and provision.

But rocks can also represent devastation and loss.

In an earlier chapter I mentioned spending forty-five days hiking to a local river where God reminded me of his promises. He spoke to me through Matthew 7 and promised me his *good bread* of provision and joy.

But that's not the whole story.

A year earlier, I had been in the throes of a painful break-up. I had dragged a heavy rock down the hill and let it fall into the center of that same river. It was a rock of pain and surrender to the Lord where I laid this relationship upon the altar of God and let him do with it as he chose.

As I tumbled the heavy rock into the middle of the river, to me that stone represented death—*not resurrection.*

I had no idea that a year later I would bask in prayer at the bank of that river and hear delightful words from Matthew 7 as God promised me *good bread* for my life:

> "Which of you, if your son asks for bread, will give him a stone? Or if he asks for a fish, will give him a snake? If you, then, though you are evil, know how to give good gifts to your children, how much more will your Father in heaven give good gifts to those who ask him!" (Matthew 7:9–11).

I want to talk about one more rock.

Let's talk about the boulder that covered the tomb where Jesus's mangled and bloody body lay. That was most certainly a rock of death and darkness.

When we read about the crucifixion of Jesus, we tend to read it in light of the coming resurrection. But those who watched Jesus die experienced catastrophic loss not knowing or understanding that Jesus would triumph over death.

The days between the crucifixion of Jesus and his resurrection would have been dreadful. What must it have been like for the mother of Jesus to watch her son tortured and beaten? What was it like for her to see him experience such a gruesome death on the cross? The friends and family of Jesus were in the throes of trauma and grief surrounding his death.

The rock that was placed in front of the tomb of Christ was not one of promise and hope but a boulder of sorrow and loss.

And yet, in Luke 24, we see God turn that stone of sorrow and loss into a stone of resurrection and joy:

> On the first day of the week, very early in the morning, the women took the spices they had prepared and went to the tomb. They found the stone rolled away from the tomb, but when they entered, they did not find the body of the Lord Jesus. While they were wondering about this, suddenly two men in clothes that gleamed like lightning stood beside them. As the women bowed down with their faces to the ground, but the men said to them, "Why do you look for the living among the dead? He is not here; he has risen!" (Luke 24:1–5).

These women, adored by Jesus, were the first who felt absolutely astonished by Jesus' resurrection.

Mary Magdalene, in particular, had the wondrous experience of actually speaking with the resurrected Christ. In fact, he called her by name in John 20:16!

We can imagine Mary running, breathless, propelled by hopeful expectation. We hear her heart pounding, almost bursting with excitement, and we see the tears of joy flowing down her cheeks.

In those first precious moments, Mary knew better than anyone that the rock that had represented such sorrow had become a miraculous symbol of God's love, grace, and resurrection power. Mary's transformation from loss to elation would have been breathtaking to behold.

God doesn't abandon us in the barren wilderness, but he gives us anticipation and promise that he is doing a new thing in defiance of death.

"Do you not perceive it? Will you not give heed to it? Will you not know it?" (Isaiah 43:19 AMPC)

Resurrection life flows from the heart of God and is exceedingly abundantly beyond all that we could hope or imagine. And this is where God meets us in our trauma and grief.

The wilderness of our bereavement is not beautiful like a Colorado hike or the untamed tropical forests of Mexico. Our wilderness is *midbar*—a desert wasteland.

But God himself promises to:

- be our rock and fortress
- revive the dead stump of our life with the mere anticipation of living water
- give us reasons to commemorate his goodness and provision
- create safe passage through impossible circumstances
- give us bread instead of a snake or stone
- astound us with flowing rivers of abundance and grace
- turn surrender into promise
- transform our sorrow into elation
- turn tombstones into doorways that reveal resurrection life

So how do we make all this happen?

We don't.

The clear promise of Scripture is that God himself pours out his love and grace upon our lives. It is not we who need to hang tough or be determined. It's not our job to create the river in the desert or roll the stone away from the mouth of tomb. And certainly, we are not able to make a dead stump come to life again by only the scent of water in the air.

In all of these passages of Scripture it is God and God alone who is making the promise and who will bring it to pass. It is God who promises to give us good bread, to bring life to a dead stump of a tree, and to make a river flow in the bleak wilderness of *midbar*.

We only need to trust him and believe his Word. We can rest in his love and grace and wait on him to accomplish these things.

When resurrection life is from his hand and not from our own efforts his gifts will spring forth with immense joy, blessing, and favor. When we trust God during our journey through the wilderness, these things be a healing balm to our soul and inspire our gifts of praise to him.

My journey through grief began with the day Gary died and my story continues onward.

I opened this book with a precious memory of Gary and me sitting together on the front stairs, our gaze lingering on the purple bougainvillea that framed our iron gate.

To this day, I can vividly remember the strong sweet smell of the surrounding guavas and tropical flowers. And I see the motmot bird sitting on our mango tree.

But I also see my husband face-down on the concrete unconscious and moaning. I hear myself crying out, "Oh, Jesus, oh, Jesus, help me!" as Nathaniel begins to give him CPR.

Since that day, God has walked my children and me through unimaginable heartbreak. But he has also given us unspeakable joy.

I mentioned in the first chapter that sometimes even good things—like the beauty of our surroundings in Mexico—come with a downside.

What I didn't realize that day as I sat with Gary on the stairs—and what I've come to intimately know after his death—is that even the most horrendous losses can include beauty and a promise of new life.

If you are in a wilderness of grief, you are not alone. God is walking you through the desert and he will take you to the rivers flowing with living water. It will be one of the most difficult journeys of your life, but our God is faithful, and he is with you.

"For the Lamb in the midst of the throne will be their shepherd, and he will guide them to springs of living water, and God will wipe away every tear from their eyes" (Revelation 7:17 ESV).

About the Author

RACHEL A. MOORE is a former missionary to Mexico and co-founder of Swordmaster Ministries Inc. She and her husband Gary had been seasoned ministry leaders when he died suddenly on the mission field where they had been serving. Today Rachel mentors those who have suffered through untimely loss, putting her arms around the bereaved and walking alongside them in their journey of grief and sorrow. She also is available to speak on coping with bereavement and moving forward through grief and loss.

Rachel is a successful real estate agent and also enjoys hiking in the Colorado mountains. She has two adult children, Bethany and Nathaniel, and a daughter-in-law, Dorie. Rachel lives in Colorado Springs, Colorado. To learn more about Rachel or invite her to speak to your group, visit: rachelmooregriefsolutions.com.

CPSIA information can be obtained
at www.ICGtesting.com
Printed in the USA
LVHW030433080321
680838LV00006B/185